教育部产学合作协同育人项目："线上线下混合+智慧共享"翻译实践基地建设（202102029010）

阜阳非遗集锦
FUYANG FEIYI JIJIN

U0120319

Illustrated Collection of Fuyang Intangible Cultural Heritage

阜阳市非物质文化遗产保护中心◎编

杨　勇　薛仰望◎译

安徽师范大学出版社
ANHUI NORMAL UNIVERSITY PRESS

·芜湖·

图书在版编目(CIP)数据

  阜阳非遗集锦 = Illustrated Collection of Fuyang Intangible Cultural Heritage:英文 / 阜阳市非物质文化遗产保护中心编;杨勇,薛仰望译.— 芜湖:安徽师范大学出版社,2023.4
  ISBN 978-7-5676-5961-2

  Ⅰ.①阜… Ⅱ.①阜…②杨…③薛… Ⅲ.①非物质文化遗产—介绍—英文 Ⅳ.①G127.543

  中国版本图书馆CIP数据核字(2023)第037691号

Illustrated Collection of Fuyang Intangible Cultural Heritage　　　杨勇　薛仰望◎译
FUYANG FEIYI JIJIN

责任编辑:吴　琼　　　　　　责任校对:晋雅雯
装帧设计:王晴晴　汤彬彬　　责任印制:桑国磊
出版发行:安徽师范大学出版社
　　　　　芜湖市北京东路1号安徽师范大学赭山校区
网　　　址:http://www.ahnupress.com/
发 行 部:0553-3883578　5910327　5910310(传真)
印　　刷:江苏凤凰数码印务有限公司
版　　次:2023年4月第1版
印　　次:2023年4月第1次印刷
规　　格:700 mm×1000 mm　1/16
印　　张:13.75
字　　数:270千字
书　　号:ISBN 978-7-5676-5961-2
定　　价:42.00元

凡发现图书有质量问题,请与我社联系(联系电话:0553-5910315)

Preface

Fuyang boasts a profound history and a brilliant culture. Back in the Neolithic Period, there were human beings living here and these ancestors created a brilliant ancient civilization. During the Spring and Autumn Period (770 BC-476 BC) and Warring States Period (475 BC-221 BC), Chu Culture[1] became the mainstream culture at that time, then it clashed with and integrated with the traditional China Central Plain Culture[2]. During the Pre-Qin Period (Paleolithic Period to 221 BC), a hundred schools of thought contended and different versions flowered, which brought many cultural phenomena to ancient Fuyang. It enriched the Chinese cultural treasury to a certain extent and gave birth to the profound and far-reaching Ying-Huai Culture[3].

The unique geographical location, featured by flat terrain, crisscross rivers, distinct four seasons and rich in products, makes Fuyang carry a large population and nurture its people's rich spiritual connotation. It is also easy to observe people in Fuyang having both a warm, spirited, romantic, elegant side, but also a hard, sincere, simple, serious side after reviewing their long history. Under their rough and generous appearance,

---

[1] "Chu Culture" refers to the culture of Chu State in the Spring and Autumn Period and Warring States Period, which is an important part of Chinese civilization.

[2] "China Central Plain Culture" refers to the cultures in the middle and lower reaches of the Yellow River.

[3] "Ying-Huai Culture" refers to the culture of Fuyang.

there is often a delicacy and gentleness hidden in their heart. They don't lack of rich imaginative qualities and the diligent pursuit for the appreciation of the beauty and a better life. For thousands of years, through continuous absorption, inheritance, development, innovation and transformation of local culture, the intangible cultural heritage with unique local characteristics had formed here, such as Fuyang Paper-cut, Jieshou Painted Pottery, Yingshang Flower-drum Lantern Dance, Huaibei Bangzi Opera. At present, Fuyang has 9 state-level intangible cultural heritage items, 28 items in province-level and 77 items in municipal-level. There are 9 state-level representative heritors, 48 province-level representative heritors, 89 municipal-level representative heritors and 326 county-level representative heritors. Fuyang also owns 5 province-level intangible cultural heritage transmission and study bases, 2 transmission and study centers, 2 education transmission and study bases and 45 municipal-level training bases. Through hard work and silent dedication, these ordinary but ingenious people in Fuyang inherited and developed intangible cultural heritages, writing a splendid scroll of Ying-Huai Culture. This tradition will move forward and last forever.

Intangible cultural heritage epitomizes local historical and cultural development and represents its essence. It is of great significance to carry forward the excellent Chinese traditional culture and build the socialist core values. It is also indispensable to nourish the local people and make them present the humanistic spirit of kindness and initiative.

Standing at the new historical position, from the strategic height to retain the soul of Chinese nation, since the Eighteenth National Congress of the Communist Party of China (CPC), the Central Committee of the CPC, with Comrade Xi Jinping as its core, has made a series of important discussions and comprehensive deployment requirements in order to promote the protection of cultural and natural heritages. As an important part of the work, the protection, inheritance and development of intangible cultural heritage is a top priority. In recent years, under the high priority of the municipal party committee and government, Fuyang's Cultural Department has done a lot of fruitful work on the rescue, protection, inheritance and development of intangible cultural heritage. It has excavated a large number of intangible cultural heritage items and has found many representative heritors. The compilation and publication of this *Illustrated Collection of Fuyang Intangible Cultural Heritage* is a kind of concentrated display.

The intangible cultural heritage of Fuyang has a long history and a profound foundation. Due to the particularity of intangible cultural heritage, with the development of the times and the changes of the environment, the protection, inheritance and development of intangible cultural heritage will face more and more challenges. In line with the principle of desperately fulfilling our duty, we will try our best to make greater contributions to inherit and develop the intangible cultural heritage in Fuyang guided by the policy of "laying first importance on protection and rescue, utilizing rationally for transmitting and development"!

Editor

Content

Chapter Two State-level and Province-level Representative Heritors of Intangible Cultural Heritage Items

Figures Content

Chapter One

State-level and Province-level

Intangible Cultural Heritage Items

One Traditional Folk Art

Fuyang Paper-cut (state-level)

Peper-cut, commonly known as "cutting-flower", was a kind of purely native folk manual art in earlier years. Fuyang Paper-cut, originated in the Northern and Southern Dynasties (420-589), has a long history. According to the relevant sources, there is a description in *The Song of Mulan*[1] of the Northern Wei Dynasty (386-534) that "By the window I combed and coiffed my cloudy hair. Before the mirror I adorned my forehead with a yellow pattern." The "yellow pattern" is a simple decoration that belongs to paper-cut. The hometown of the heroine Hua Mulan[2] who "joined the army on her father's behalf" locates in the Bozhou city which is close to Fuyang city in the Northwestern Anhui province. This means that there was a prototype of paper-cut in Northwest Anhui at that time.

For its aesthetic and practical functions, Fuyang Paper-cut has a strong vitality among local people. Many illiterate farmers can hold scissors to cut out simple and generous cutting works in the shape of shoes, pillow, hat, bib, costume, Chinese characters " 喜 " (represent happiness) and "寿"(represent longevity) in order to use or sell. The paper-cut can be learnt or discussed from family members and handed down by private families or villages as units. In the Fuyang Museum, there are some works of paper-cut from the Qing Dynasty (1636-1912) such as *Blue*

---

[1] *The Song of Mulan* is a long narrative poem.

[2] Hua Mulan, a heroine in ancient China. She joined the army on behalf of her father and defeated the invading nation.

Bridge, *Pastoral Flute* and *Sacrificial Pagoda*. These works have reached a high artistic level, featured by clear cutting-edge technique, simple composition and rich imagination.

In the long course of development, Fuyang Paper-cut absorbed a lot of folk culture nutrients through continuous processing and innovation of craftsmen. It also borrowed from external cutting methods, thus forming unique and charming artistic characteristics. Compared with other paper-cut schools nationwide, Fuyang Paper-cut has distinctive regional characteristics. In terms of cutting techniques, it mainly uses scissors to cut lines to represent patterns supplemented by faces; In terms of patterns, it doesn't pursue the details of patterns, but seeks for the expression and image. By attaching great importance on the changes of contour, the work shows its features with bold and bombastic style, ingenious design and simple patterns; In terms of composition, it pays less attention to the blueprint. Artists are likely to composite in their clear mind. At the same time, they pay attention to the changes of the lines' thickness to achieve the transition of layers from black to white and gray. With these mutual contrasts, the gradation is distinct and the patterns are full, compact and full of tension; In terms of production processes, it borrows the expression of the print lines whose processing pays heed to the changes of the lines in order to reflect the strength and texture of the lines. Through the smooth outline of lines, it reflects the artistic effect of simpleness and exaggeration. In the process of paper-cutting, the paper often turns with the scissors. Many patterns are often appeared along with the suspending of scissors in one paper without mending, which shows the charm of paper-cutting. The creator and the admirer can get great artistic enjoyment from the process of production; In terms of decoration methods, it pays attention to the graphic structure of patterns with various decoration techniques, such as folding and shearing decoration, arc external serration decoration, opening decoration, perspective decoration, vortex pattern decoration, which are different from paper-cut in other places.

A unique region nurtures its people and local unique folk culture and art. Fuyang is located at the north-south climate dividing line, featuring flat and vast terrain. People in here are honest and kind. Paper-cut reflects the Ying-Huai folk customs with regional cultural elements in it. As people here have both the briskness and generosity of the northerners, and the delicacy and carefulness of the southerners, the paper-cutting works are naturally branded with natives' characters which are showed by boldness within attentiveness, unconventional appearance, natural free in deep sincereness, soft heart under the strength, delicacy in simple livelihood and subtlety within roughness.

The work is the epitome of life. For its vividness, Fuyang Paper-cut gains much people's favor and market demand. There are also many people who depend on paper-cut for a living. At present, Fuyang Paper-cut is gaining more and more momentum of development with a good rate. The talent pool is made up of rationally different generations with orderly transmission. Traditional paper-cut and paper-stenciling coexist in terms of techniques. The content of paper-cut is rich and colorful. The performance themes can be flora and fauna, scenes and stories of people's daily life, scenic spots, zodiac animals, folklore and literature, opera and folk customs, utensils and supplies, etc. These themes can meet various aesthetic needs. Companies specializing in paper-cut have also emerged.

Fuyang's Cultural Department attaches great importance to the cultivation of talents. Each county and district have their own paper-cut team. Fuyang Normal University and local vocational schools establish paper-cutting courses. More than 60 urban and rural Children's Palaces own paper-cut training courses. Yingzhou district is awarded the title of "the hometown of Paper-cut". Feng Gicai, the vice chairman of the Chinese Federation of Literary and Art Circles, and the chairman of the Chinese Folk Artists Association, once praised Fuyang Paper-cut in a poem, "The hands are agile and ingenious; the mind is wise and intelligent. The paper rotates with the cutting of scissors; all the patterns are created in a moment."

Fig 1 The Collection of Paper-cut Works

During historical development and cumulative experience, a group of influential artists and heritors have emerged in Fuyang Paper-cut. Cheng Jianli's works won national gold medal six times, and he was awarded the title of "Master of Folk Arts and Crafts"; Wang Jiahe has been engaged in paper-cut for 70 years, and is known as the "Treasure Bag" of folk paper-cut; Such artists, as Lv Fengmao, Jia Peixiu have played an active role in the development and transmission of paper-cut; Cheng Xinghong, a state-level heritor, and Liu Jicheng, Ge Tingyou, Wu Qingping and Ren Huaijian, province-level heritors, etc., have made outstanding achievements. Today, Fuyang Paper-cut has become an important cultural postcard to carry the reputation of "great and beautiful Fuyang" to the nation and beyond.

In June 2008, Fuyang Paper-cut entered the second list of state-level intangible cultural heritage representative items.

Huanggang Willow Weaving (state-level)

Huanggang Willow Weaving has a long history. Its raw materials, Qi willow (a kind of willow) has been planted for thousand years and its weaving history also can be traced to 500 years ago. According to the historical documents of Funan county, there are large areas of tidal flats and wetlands on the both sides of Huai River and Hong River, in which much wet-loving willows grows there. These willlows are suitable for weaving. *Yingzhou Annals* of the Zhengde Period (1506-1521) of Ming Dynasty records that "Huaibei and Mengcheng (two places) were rich in "shuijin" (people called Qi willow as "shuijin" at that time). People logged and processed willows. These willows were white as jade and tough as rattan." People always said that weaving willows in the shape of baskets was to support the family. There was a tradition of relying on waving Qi willow to make some simple daily necessities for sale since ancient times in the areas along the Huai River with Huanggang town as the center. Since the late Ming Dynasty and the early Qing Dynasty (1600-1644), local businessmen will hold temple fairs at the end of the third lunar month, mainly to expand the trade of raw materials and the products of willow weaving. Over times, Huanggang, with its relatively convenient water and land transportation, has gradually become a well-known distribution center of willow weaving products. Later, the "willow weaving street" came into being here.

Fig 2 The Collection of Huanggang Willow Weaving Products

Qi willow is unique in texture. After processing, the wicker becomes soft, easy to bend and difficult to fold with uniform thickness and elegant color. In the process of weaving, folk craftsmen had developed a set of traditional techniques. According to the materials, later generations have applied these techniques and constantly improved them for producing practical and beautiful utensils that are close to people's life. In modern times, people in Huanggang are far away home to promote sales of their products, learn skills, and bring back new design conception and weaving technology. This promotes the new development of willow weaving industry. The new techniques of willow weaving mainly include "pingbian" (intertwined weaving), "wenbian" (intertwined weaving with straited pattern), "lebian" (trussing weaving by using hemp rope), "qibian" (piling weaving by using bamboo stripe to pile fabrics up) and "chanbian" (winding weaving for decoration and fixing). By improving the material processing technology and updating the design conception, local people can weave all kinds of simple, natural, beautiful, light and durable practical products at will.

Fig 3 Willow Weaving Products Waiting for Sale

In the early 1950s, Huanggang town established the Willow Weaving Cooperative. In 1973, Yang ruzeng, Yang Shuqing and others founded the willow weaving factory. At present, many willow weaving companies have been established in the town, making these products become the local bulk industry and the main export brand of Northwest Anhui. Now, Qi willow are planted for one hundred thousand Mu (more than 6000 hectares) in Huanggang area, driving tens of thousands of people around into the willow weaving occupation to get rid of poverty and become prosperous. After the reform and opening up (1978), with the liberalization of the market, people in Huanggang use their indomitable spirit to blaze new trails to take willow products out of the countryside to the city, out of the mainland to the coast, out of home to abroad. Under the guidance of the local government, willow weaving has become a kind of unique artwork by training technicians and improving varieties. In 1978, Huanggang Willow Weaving took part in the First Canton Fair, which attracted the attention of domestic and foreign merchants and was widely favored. Liu Tingxin and others also became the first group of farmers of Huanggang to produce willow weaving products jointly with foreign merchants. After 1980, with the rise of township enterprises, Huanggang Willow Weaving entered a rapid development period. After 1985, the average annual output of willow weaving products increased by 23.8%.

After willow weaving went abroad, there was also higher requirements for weaving technology and product quality. Using oriental wisdom and ingenuity, people in Huanggang weave handicrafts in various forms. In terms of type, there are furniture decoration series, flower basket series, fruit basket series, basket series, laundry basket series, tourism and leisure series, pet basket series; In terms of style, there are dozens of floral baskets used for daily life, simple usage, tri-color decoration and double-mouth container, ranging from small to several inches. There are thousands kinds of baskets, such as fruit baskets, paper baskets, towel baskets, decorative baskets; In terms of color, there are not only pure and white light baskets, but also colorful baskets. Among them, the white ones look like snow with red ones gorgeous, yellow ones bright and black ones deep; In terms of usage, there are various willow weaving products. Some of them are plates for holding bread, fruit and sugar. Some of them are bookshelves to place books and newspapers. Some of them are vases for inserting flowers and so on. These products are widely used in all aspects of life. Besides, weaving techniques of "libian" (three-dimensional weaving), "jingbian" (warp weaving), "ningbian" (weaving through twisting after twisting) and "weaving by using wild red rattan" in Huanggang are at the first-class level nationwide. There are also many skillful craftsmen whose craftsmanship and products are fabulous. The largest automatic production line for deep processing products of willow weaving in China is established here, which can produce twenty categories and tens of thousands of varieties of products. These products are placed into supermarkets, exported to more than 60 countries and regions, such as Western Europe, North America, East Asia, Southeast Asia, the Middle East, Hong Kong, Macao and Taiwan. Some of the larger domestic willow weaving dealers also like to order products from Huanggang and then resell them to other places.

The value of Huanggang Willow Weaving lies in that it not only provides a lot of convenience for people's life, but also can be appreciated as an elegant artwork. More importantly, the product conforms to the modern people's consumption conception of paying attention to green and environmental protection. It also has a broad development prospect. Given this, Funan county is also known as "the hometown of Qi willow in

China", "the hometown of Chinese willow weaving" and "the hometown of Chinese folk culture and art".

In May 2011, Huanggang Willow Weaving entered the third list of state-level intangible cultural heritage representative items.

Du Style Copper Engraving (state-level)

Du Style Copper Engraving was created in the Republic of China (1912-1949) by Mr. Du Xingjing (his ancestral home is located at Chahua town, Yingdong district, Fuyang city). In the late Qing Dynasty (1840-1912), Du Xingjing studied copper engraving techniques in the capital and learned from the master of copper carving, Mr. Chen Yinsheng. After that, Du Hongnian, the second-generation heritor of Du Style Copper Engraving, innovated on the basis of inheriting Chen Yinsheng's copper engraving techniques, and integrated print techniques into the copper carving techniques to form his own techniques.

Fig 4 The Collection of Du Style Copper Engraving Works

It can be traced back to the art of engraving copper in the Spring and Autumn and Warring States Period (770 BC-221) when we review the copper engraving techniques. Du Style Copper Engraving inherited and developed this ancient craft, which can be viewed as the reappearance and innovation of traditional copper engraving. Among three generations of

Du's family, each generation inherited ancestors' techniques while not complacent and conservative. Through each generation's efforts, Du Style Cooper Engraving inherited and innovated traditional techniques such as "yinke" (engraving the patterns or characters inward), "yangke" (engraving the patterns or characters into outward), "shenzhuo" (engraving deeply), "shuanggouxian" (engraving silhouette by using lines), "mashengxian" (engraving patterns or characters by using twines) and "maodiao" (engraving delicately in gold and silver flakes). Through the combination of various techniques, the product seeks to perform the perfect effect. Every work of Du Style Copper Engraving is exquisite, delicate, and refined, which has high artistic value.

Du Style Copper Engraving is a kind of manual art, which uses self-made special engraving knife and white copper and brass as the main materials. From many processes, such as material selection, script finalization, engraving, polishing, baking, the patterns are emerged on the copper surface. Du Style Copper Engraving absorbs the traditional bamboo engraving, inlay carving, seal carving and other folk techniques. The main engraving utensils include ink cartridge, paperweight, fumigation oven, tea box, teapot, hookah bag, wine vessel, plate, etc., among which ink cartridge is the most famous. The main themes are landscapes, figures, flowers and birds, etc. In terms of operation technology, it is a kind of engraving with great difficulty and superb technology. The work is a folk "copper painting" craft with deep, magnificent and elegant charm.

The main objects of Du Style Copper Engraving are articles for amusement. The main engraving patterns are calligraphy and painting seals which are very scholarly. Therefore, there are higher requirements for the producer's creation level for calligraphy and painting as well as cultural and artistic accomplishment. The composition and material selection of the work not only have traditional themes, but also reflect the current situation of contemporary social life, folk customs, cultural and artistic achievements, and historical events and figures. Therefore, Du Style Copper Engraving has a profound historical and cultural connotation and high collection value, which has become an art treasure favored by scholars and collectors.

From Mr. Du Xingjing, the first-generation heritor, Du Style Copper Engraving technology has a history of more than 100 years. Du family moves forward in groping. Especially the third-generation heritor, Mr. Du Ping, he learned this art from his father when he was young, carried forward this endangered item through his exquisite craftmanship and skillful techniques. Through observing the changes of the depth and thickness of patterns, he outlined and engraved many images which are penetrating in depth and delicate in surface. He further broadened the theme of engraving, which are mainly painting or calligraphy. He also wrote famous aphorisms, poems and proses on the copper. In recent years, he has created many excellent works. Since his works have won the silver medal in the First Anhui Folk Craft Exhibition in 2007, more than 100 works have won awards issued by the Ministry of Culture of China and province departments. Among them, *National Soul* and *The Birth of New China* are representative works. At present, his works have a great influence in Northern Anhui and become one of the most exquisite and representative folk handicrafts in this area. His works and influence spread from Fuyang to Northern Anhui, even to Eastern Henan province and Jiangsu province, with more and more learners following him.

In November 2014, Du Style Copper Engraving entered the fourth list of state-level intangible cultural heritage representative items.

Jieshou Embroidery (province-level)

Jieshou Embroidery is a kind of folk embroideries that combines "flat stitch" (a kind of knitting skill) technique and the art of clothes in northern China areas with a long history. As early as the Warring States Period (475 BC-221 BC), Xincheng (an ancient city) was built in Jieshou, and embroidery crafts began to flourish. It can be testified by gold thread embroidered official uniforms and clothing unearthed from the tombs at that time. Since then, the folk embroidery technology integrated the northern and southern techniques. In the Tang (618-907) and Song (960-1279) Dynasties, Jieshou Embroidery formed its unique style.

Jieshou Embroidery has unique needling techniques, such as "tioahua" (stitch method that strictly accordance with the fabric warp and weft pattern), "jiahua" (one-side stitch), "qianhua" (two-sides stitch), "duanmian xiuhua" (stitch flowers on satin), "butie xiuhua" (stitch patterns on clothes). It belongs to folk flat stitch embroidery. The colors are bright red, green and purple. It is mainly made of gold and silver thread, with yellow, red and green satins, decorated with various metal pieces and gold spikes, making the embroidery more delicate.

Fig 5 The Embroidered Hats and Shoes

As a folk craft, Jieshou Embroidery stems from traditional farming culture. Its pattern design is mostly from flowers and plants, insects and fish, birds and animals, and even natural landscape, as well as figures from operas and legends. The composition is based on lines, combined with faces, striving to complement each other in artistic conception, situation and charm. Most of the contents are to describe the people's pursuit for a happy life, reflecting the expectation of long life for their descendants and longing for peace and auspiciousness. Using flat stitch as the main method, the embroidery chooses gold thread to connect the lace so as to highlight the visual sense of color. The patterns are mainly composed of plants, animals and figures.

During the Anti-Japanese War (1931-1945), due to special historical and environmental reasons, Jieshou was once known as "a little Shanghai" in the rear battlefield. In addition, with its developed water transportation, Jieshou attracted merchants gathered here and the economy developed rapidly. During this period, the large market demand and the improvement of people's appreciation level contributed the development and quality of Jieshou Embroidery. At that time, the embroidery products were famous for the embroidered hats and shoes produced by three sisters of Dai family, which were known as "Dai style embroidery".

After the founding of the People's Republic of China, Jieshou Embroidery got partial recovery. The traditional colors of bright red, green and purple have been continued. The materials used for silk and accessories are symmetrical. The works include vamp, toe cap, clothes, gloves, pillows, etc., which are favored by the masses. In the 1880s, Liu Lanying, the representative heritor of Jieshou Embroidery, reformed and innovated this craft, integrating the strengths of northern and southern Chinese embroidery schools. The experts praised her works as the masterpiece of embroidery. In 1985, her works won the excellent award in the National Folk Arts and Crafts Exhibition with feature story reported by the CCTV and province TV stations. In 2009, she was invited to give a lecture in Macao, and her embroidery works were deeply loved by the Macao people.

At present, Jieshou Embroidery has formed a school featured by the combination of flat stitch technique and the art of clothes with Liu Lanying as the representative. There are also many talents, mainly distributed in more than 200 villages such as Xicheng, Shuzhuang, Daiqiao, Guji, Quanyang, Guangwu and other towns. The needlework techniques have great influence in Fuyang city, Taihe county, Linquan county and Zhoukou city of Henan province, and the products are sold at home and abroad.

In July 2010, Jieshou Embroidery entered the third list of province-level intangible cultural heritage representative items.

Xiyang Embroidery (province-level)

Known as Xiyang in ancient times, Taihe is a county with a long history and profound culture. The folk culture here is rich and diverse with Fuyang (Xiyang) Embroidery as one of the representatives.

According to archaeological research, ancient Xiyang, also known as Juyang, was the capital of Chu State[1] for 12 years, which lies in Ruiyang village, Gongji town of Taihe county now. The techniques of Xiyang Embroidery should had introduced into the folk from the palace of Chu State at that time, and got inheritance and development. Thus, Xiyang Embroidery has a broad mass base.

Fig 6 Cat-head-like Shoes and Tiger-head-like Cap

Near the Shaying River, Taihe county is located at the Central Plains[2] which is the intersection areas of Chinese cultures. In the course of development, Xiyang Embroidery absorbed the essence of northern and southern embroidery techniques, forming its own unique style. Its products integrate the richness of Yue Embroidery, the delicacy of Shu Embroidery, the dignity of Jing Embroidery, the beauty and charm of Su Embroidery, and the ruggedness and simplicity of Bian Embroidery. The products of

---

[1] "Chu State" refers to a feudal state along the Yangtze River in the Pre-Qin Dynasty (Paleolithic period to 221 BC).

[2] "the Central Plains" refers to the middle and lower reaches of the Yellow River.

Xiyang Embroidery are exquisite and structured, with bright colors, powerful patterns, beautiful images and firm texture, which are favored by people at all levels and has been handed down for thousands of years.

Xiyang Embroidery has a unique craft production in Northern Anhui. The level of its production techniques has a certain historical reference value for the study of the natural economy and social productivity at that time. Xiyang Embroidery has rich connotation and distinctive features. The patterns are simple, elegant and auspicious with more metaphorical symbolic figures used. Among them, flowers, insects and birds are used to express people's praying for good fortune without misfortune; The embroidery with the themes of happiness, wealth and longevity is mostly used for the elderly, praying for their health and longevity; The embroidery designed for children with the themes of lion, tiger, the five poisonous creatures (scorpion, viper, centipede, house lizard, toad) and so on is used to avoid and suppress evil; The embroidery designed for newly married couple adopts the patterns such as mandarin duck playing in the water, a baby along with the lotus and carps playing with lotus, which implies family harmony and more children bringing more happiness.

Xiyang Embroidery integrates the strengths of northern and southern embroidery, but still retains the original hand-made techniques with a strong local flavor. Since the new era, the products have been widely favored through its inheritance, development and technological innovation. The heritor, Yuan Yuling's works such as *Shawls*, *Cat-head-like Shoes* and *Tiger-head-like Cap* won prizes in Folk Handicraft Exhibitions held in Singapore, Macao and other countries and regions. Many of her works have been collected by embroidery lovers at home and abroad.

In July 2010, Xiyang Embroidery entered the third list of province-level intangible cultural heritage representative items.

Linquan Gourd Pyrography (province-level)

Linquan Gourd Pyrography has a long history, which can be traced back to the late Qing Dynasty (1840-1912). Li Yanggao, a native of Huaji town of Linquan county, is not only a famous calligrapher and painter, but also the founder of Linquan Gourd Pyrography.

Fig 7 The Electric Soldering Procedure

Li Haoxian, Li Zhaolin, Li Dingbin, Li Zhenyu, these descendants of Li Yanggao, with these heritors Niu Diankui and Liu Lihai, etc., they carried forward this kind of rare ancient pyrography technique from generations to generations, and gradually applied the electric soldering iron technology to the creation of gourd pyrography. The couple Li Zhenyu and Han Yumei, the fifth-generation heritors, have been insisted to inherit this ancient folk art under extremely difficult living conditions for decades. They have gradually developed a traditional family workshop into a handicraft company which includes planting, production, publicity, marketing, talent training and research of gourd pyrography. They have carried forward this native folk handicraft and made remarkable achievements.

Compared with the schools of gourd pyrography in Jiangsu province,

Zhejiang province, Shanxi province, Shandong province and other places, Linquan Gourd Pyrography has the distinct regional characteristics of primitive simplicity, ruggedness and generousness. It has brilliant techniques which include traditional Chinese painting techniques such as line drawing, fine brushwork, freehand brushwork. By using these techniques, it creates vivid patterns of figures, landscape, flowers and birds, animals on the smooth and hard surface of gourd. Its production is exquisite with many procedures, such as design and mapping, drawing through following the sample, clear painting and finalization, electric soldering, revamping and lacquering, and drying in the shade. Among them, electric soldering also needs many fine procedures, such as drawing the outline, wiping the texture, drawing finely and dotting with ink. There are high requirements for the artist's skills, such as the control of temperature and time, brush strength, speeding skills.

For hundreds of years, Linquan Gourd Pyrography has been inherited continuously. It spreads to Anhui province, Henan province, Shandong province and other areas with Linquan county as the center. The products have won prizes in many exhibitions (competitions), which are very popular among the people.

In November 2017, Linquan Gourd Pyrography entered the fifth list of province-level intangible cultural heritage representative items.

Two Traditional Opera

Huaibei Bnagzi Opera (state-level)

Huaibei Bangzi Opera, formerly known as Bangzi Opera, also known as Shahe Tune, is called as Bangzi for short. As one of the most influential local operas, it has a long history and is widely spread to Fuyang city, Huaibei city and Huainan city of Anhui province, even to Shangqiu city, Zhoukou city and Luohe city of Henan province and Xuzhou city of Jiangsu province.

Originated from Bangzi Operas of Shanxi province and Shaanxi province, Huaibei Bnagzi Opera had formed through several large-scale migrations from Shanxi. During the late Ming and early Qing Period (1600-1644), the frequent warfare of the Northwest Peasant Army[①] on both sides of the Huai River, along with the rise of merchants of Shanxi and Shaanxi in the economically developed Ying-Huai area at that time, lay the foundation for the development and market demand of Bangzi Opera. Later, Bangzi Opera absorbed the local popular folk tunes such as "zhuiziweng" (an ancient traditional opera), "zhaowangxi" (an opera with the theme of Kitchen God), "Huai Tune" (an ancient traditional opera), "budaixi" (an opera by using puppet to perform) and "chuagong haozi" (Boatman's singing songs) along the Sha River area. Through the arrangement, innovation and combination of local dialect and tunes, artists produced Shahe Opera which serves as the predecessor of today's Huaibei Bangzi Opera.

---

① "the Northwest Peasant Army" refers to the uprising army to against the taxation of the imperial court.

Shahe Opera, also known as "rustic Bangzi" and "high-pitched tune", together with Yingshang Flower-drum Lantern Dance, have become two popular folk-art forms in Northern and Southern China areas. At that time, the saying was that "When performing, if you want to change the tune, you have to choose between Northern and Southern tune-patterns. The content of Southern tune-pattern is Flower-drum Lantern Dance and the content of Northern-pattern is Bangzi Opera." The scale of performance in that period was not large. There was a saying that "in a troupe, there are only three sets of costumes, a costume for the emperor called "mang", an armor costume for the general called "kao", and a costume for the civil servant called "guanyi", accompanying with one flute and half of cymbals". In the middle and late Qing Dynasty (1736-1912), due to the opening of various classes (for opera training) and troupes, a large number of performing talents were cultivated, which made this opera be carried forward, developed and optimized. This also became a popular opera among the people in Northern Anhui. Among these classes, there was an influential class called "elite class of Shahe Tune" which was run by Shen Wankui of Weizhai town, Linquan county. His class flourished during the Daoguang reign (1821-1850) by using the way of teaching and learning at the same time. In the 23rd year of Guangxu reign (1897), Zhou Dianchen, a wujuren[1] of Tupo town, Linquan county, founded another "elite class of Shahe Tune". His class was also known as "class of wujuren", which had a far-reaching influence and cultivated many famous actors of Bangzi Opera. These actors include red face[2]

---

[1] "wujuren" refers to the military successful candidate in the imperial provincial examination.

[2] "red face" refers to a kind of face painting in the performance of operas, traditionally for the heroic or the honest.

named Mei Hu and black face[1] named Wang Nian. The later "three representatives of Huaibei Bangzi Opera", Zhu Jilin (stage name: Zhudabizi), Wang Dengke (stage name: Wangdayan), Gu Qun (stage name: Guxixuan), also graduated from the "class of wujuren". Among them, Gu Qun is not only an influential artist, but also a senior who played an active role in the transmission of Huaibei Bangzi Opera. His "Gu's training class" established on both sides of the Sha River of Jieshou city, which had a far-reaching impact. By the middle and late 1930s, the opera training classes founded in Fuyang had sprung up and cultivated plenty of performing talents.

In the process of development, Huaibei Bangzi Opera had formed its distinctive roles which can be divided into four categories. They are male in general, female in general, clowns and facial design. The tune is not only high pitched, rough, bold, but also soft, deep, simple and generous. The libretto is regular, emphasizing level and oblique tones as well as rhythm. The plate-type[2] of structure of this opera was greatly influenced by Henan Opera because it is close to Henan province. At first, it sounds like Henan Opera, but there are obvious differences after careful listening. The performance of Huaibei Bangzi Opera is full of local flavor. The performance is simple, warm and unrestrained with exaggerated actions, many coloraturas, prolongated tunes and strong rhythm.

---

[1] "black face" also refers to a kind of face painting in the performance of operas, traditionally for the figure who is honest, impartial, brave, or reckless.

[2] "plate-type" is a kind of structural style in Chinese opera and quyi music.

Fig 8 The Performing Pictures

The repertoire of Huabei Bangzi Opera is divided into old plays (traditional opera) and new plays (modern opera). There are more than 700 traditional plays, and more than 600 of them are performed regularly. The themes of these traditional plays are mostly taken from the collection of classics and history, literature, folklore, etc. The content is mainly to publicize loyalty, filial piety, justice and what goes around comes around. The plays often give full play to the singing skills of actors, which are easy to understand with strong pedagogical meaning. For example, the plays, such as *Appealing in the Court, Hanging for Filial Piety* and *Immolating* have a great influence on shaping the moral values of the public.

After the founding of the People's Republic of China, the CPC and the government attached great importance to the development of Huaibei Bangzi Opera. Relevant departments of Fuyang set up a specialized group to research the performance, creative talents, repertoire, plays and so on. They also put these data on files for protection. These increasingly efforts of excavation and collation have gained fruitful results. In 1960, plays *Boots on Kou Zhun's Back* and *Eulogizing the Nian Army* were performed in Beijing, which were well-received. In 1962, Anhui Film Studio adapted the play *Boots on Kou Zhun's Back* with Gu Qun as the protagonist, and appointed Xu Jianhua and Wan Yizhou to finish the film script. This play was reproduced into a dramatic art film and screened nationwide, further expanding the influence of Huaibei Bangzi Opera.

Since the reform and opening up, folk opera, as an important part of the policy of rejuvenating city through culture, has been on the stage of the times. This ancient opera, Huaibei Bangzi Opera, has regained its vitality. Many talents have come out and their works have taken part in major municipal and provincial art activities. Some of them, such as *Painting Tiger, Outside the Window, Lives of Three Women, An Infatuated Girl and a Heartless Man, Dressing and Making up* won the first prize of Provincial Sketch Competitions, Drama Performances and Exhibitions. In 2007, the newly created play *Nightmare* participated in the Eighth Provincial Culture and Art Festival and won the excellent play award; In 2013, the newly created play *Yingchun Sisiter* won the excellent play award of the Tenth Provincial Art Festival and the thirteenth provincial "excellent works in five aspects" award; In 2016, the play *Blooming Flowers and Full Moon* won the fifteenth China population culture award, the fourteenth provincial "excellent works in five aspects" award and Tian Han drama award (play award and script Award); In 2018, the newly created play *Forever Dabie Mountain* won the national excellent play award of Bangzi Tunes sponsored by the Propaganda Department of the CPC Central Committee and the Ministry of Culture and Tourism.

In May 2011, Huaibei Bnagzi Opera entered the third list of state-level intangible cultural heritage representative items.

Funan Haizi Opera (state-level)

Haizi Opera, also known as Heizi opera, begins with a prolonged tune which sounds like Chinese pronunciation "Hai". During the performance, the opera also needs to use "Hai" to fix the tune, hit the beat and prolong the tune when singing the libretto. This is the origin of the name of "Haizi". It is one of the representative local traditional operas in Anhui province.

Originated in Funan county which is located on the bank of Huai River, Haizi Opera gains popularity in Funan county, Yingshang county, Gushi county, Huaibin county and Shangcheng county. It was formed from Jiaqing reign (1795-1820) to Daoguang reign (1821-1850) of Qing Dynasty. According to archaeological research, after some folk dances such as Huatiao Dance[1], Red Lantern Dance[2], Land Boat Dance[3] finished, artists used to perform some coloraturas, operas or folk songs in addition. Later, these extra performances developed into "liangxiaoxi" (an opera only with two-roles performance) and "sanxiaoxi" (an opera only with three-roles performance), then gradually into a real opera and even a continuous opera with connected stories. They were mainly active in the middle and upper reaches of Huai River.

Funan county is the discovery site of state-level treasure "Dragon-and-Tiger Bronze Ware". It is also the birthplace of contemporary "Spirit

---

[1] "Huatiao Dance" refers to a kind of dance that a woman shoulders a thin and flexible bamboo pole with colored stripes on it and bamboo basket hanging at both ends. When performing, this woman takes this "huatiao" (bamboo pole) to dance.

[2] "Red Lantern Dance" has similar form with the "Huatiao Dance", but with red lanterns hanging at both ends.

[3] "Land Boat Dance" refers to a kind of folk dance that simulates sailing in water.

of Wangjiaba①". With splendid and profound history and culture and the moving spirit in the new era, people here have an innate love for art. In 1958, Haizi Opera troupe was established. Zhou Xuezhong, an opera teacher, sorted out and processed the tunes of Haizi Opera by adding orchestral music and percussion music. He trained performing talents, collected and adopted traditional plays for the creation of new plays. He also organized public performances. Through these efforts, Haizi Opera had its first development period. In the 1950s and 1960s, Funan Haizi Opera performed more than 280 times a year. At the beginning of reform and opening up, there were more than 300 performances per year, which had a great influence in Anhui province and Henan province which are located in the middle and upper reaches of Huai River.

During the performance of Funan Haizi Opera, local dialect is used with flexible forms. The tune of Haizi Opera belongs to "Yiyang Tune" (a kind of traditional opera tune) and is also influenced by "Yuyao Tune" (another traditional opera tune). It is mainly composed of "Banqiang Style" (a form of structural style in Chinese opera and quyi), supplemented by "Qupai" (a kind of accompaniment). It is also combined with assistant chanting, forming the characteristic of singing, assistant chanting and beating in one opera. The tune is not only divided into roles of male in general, female in general, the painted face, and clowns, but also divided into speed of fastness and slowness. The five-tone② scales are often used in the singing, with some six-tone scales. Sometimes, they also

---

① "Spirit of Wangjiaba" refers to the spirit of taking care of the overall situation at the expense of personal interests, the spirit of self-improvement without afraid of difficulties and danger and the spirit of unity between the army and the people.

② "five-tone" refers to ancient tonality of Han nationality. It starts from "Gong" (equals Do) to "Yu" (equals So).

have the characteristic of appoggiatura with degrees of "gong" (equals Do), "zhi" (equals Re) and "yu" (equals So). Its singing style is lively, bright and interesting, which can be divided into two categories of main tunes and coloraturas (miscellaneous tunes). The main tunes include "laoshengdiao" (high-pitched melody singing by man), "xiwazi" (simple and bright melody to express the joy of young men and women) and "kuwazi" (melody to sing the sad and painful feeling of the characters) and so on. The coloraturas are selected from some plays, such as *Go to Shaanxi*, *Go to Chenzhou*, *Pagoda*. Most of the librettos adopt basic sentences which include ten-characters sentence, eight-characters sentence, seven-characters sentence, six-characters sentence, five-characters sentence, four-characters sentence, three-characters sentence, etc. Haizi Opera has high tunes, with distinct local characteristics.

Fig 9 The Performing Pictures of Modern Plays

In 2007, Funan county established the protection committee of Haizi Opera, which further strengthened the protection and inheritance of this opera. Up to now, more than 130 traditional plays have been excavated and sorted out. Among them, more than 20 plays are often performed, such as *Beating Peach Blossom*, *Standing Near The Flower Wall*, and *Squire Wang Discarded His Wife*. More than 40 new plays have created, among which *One Millionth of a Second* and *Obstinate Captain* are the representatives.

In 2009, *The Spirit of Wangjiaba* was created and rehearsed, which was well-received after the public performance; In 2015, Haizi Opera Art School of Funan county adapted the play, *History of Revolutionaries* to participate in the local opera performance of the National Vocational Skills Competition; In 2016, Cultural Center of Funan county adapted the play, *Doing as required*, which won the gold award of the Thirteenth Opera and Sketch Competition held by six provinces and one city in Eastern China; In 2018, *Bidding*, created and rehearsed by Funan Performing Arts Center, participated in the opera performance of national grassroots troupes sponsored by the Propaganda Department of the CPC Central Committee and the Ministry of Culture and Tourism in Beijing.

In May 2011, Funan Haizi Opera entered the third list of state-level intangible cultural heritage representative items.

Yingshang Tui Opera (province-level)

Yingshang Tui opera, also known as "Four-sentence Tui Opera", is a local opera of Anhui province, and belongs to one of the rare national operas.

Originated from folk small tunes, Yingshang Tui Opera formed with the development of Yingshang Flower-drum Lantern Dance. At the beginning of the 20th century, Tang Peijin, the heritor of Yingshang Huagu Opera, created "Four-sentence Tui Opera" for the first time in the process of reform and innovation of Flower-drum Lantern Dance. After the performance, this art became popular. Later, after generations of artists' re-inheritance and new development, this art became an independent type of opera, Yingshang Tui Opera.

Yingshang Tui Opera has distinctive features. The tunes are composed of five-scales, which are euphemistic, lyrical, fluent and lively; The narrative-singing parts in an opera adopts local dialect, which are close to people; The performance inherits the movements and footwork of Flower-drum Lantern Dance. Its classical meaning is obvious with rich local flavor. The masses are easy to understand, sing, and learn this opera. Once produced, it has been widely spread.

In the early period, Yingshang Tui Opera was mostly a playlet at the end of Flower-drum Lantern Dance. The roles were mainly male in general and female in general. The plays were mainly composed by *Child Cowherd, Big Pot, Green Snake and White Snake Love Xu Xian, Dongbin Plays Peony* and so on. After that, through the processing and arrangement of the artists, this opera absorbed folk songs, opera music and quyi, later became a comprehensive culture and art which integrates opera, dance and music. There were excellent plays appearing such as *Farewell Xiangcha*,

The Story of Tea Bottle, Li Tianbao Borrows Grain.

Fig 10 The Performance of a Female Role

In 1952, the troupe of Yingshang Tui Opera was established by the county government. Most of the newly created plays are in praise of new China and all kinds of heroes as well as the achievements of socialist construction. After entering the new era, Yingshang Tui Opera has been further inherited and developed. Some plays such as *Antiphon in the New Year*, *Farewell My Beloved*, *Return Home Together*, and *Go to Temple Fair* are often performed everywhere. The main artists are Tang Peijin, Wu Liqin (stage name: diaobayouchui), Wang Chuanxian (stage name: yitiaobian), Zhang Shaobai (stage name: baisuizi), and Wang Yun (stage name: lalating). Their performances are spread in Yingshang county, Lixin county of Fuyang city, Fengtai county, Huainan city and Shou county, which are well-received by the audience. Yingshang Tui Opera has a long history and rich connotation, which has a certain reference value for the study of the evolution of folk songs, dances and opera music in Huai River.

In December 2006, Yingshang Tui Opera entered the first list of province-level intangible cultural heritage representative items.

Northern Anhui Qu Opera (province-level)

Formerly known as "Stilt Opera", "Opera with small tunes" and "Tune Opera", Northern Anhui Qu Opera has strong artistic individuality, serving as one of the most popular local operas that spreads Northwest Anhui with Fuyang as the center.

At the end of the Qing Dynasty and the beginning of the Republic of China (1900-1920), Guzi Tune, a kind of opera that combines Jieshou Yugu (a kind of percussion instrument), Zhuiziweng (an ancient traditional opera) and other folk tunes with folk stilts and dance, was popular in the rural areas between Anhui province, Henan province and Shandong province. Later, this tune finally moved to the local opera stage in 1934 after street-to-street performances.

The tune structure of Northern Anhui Qu Opera is "Qupai Style" (a kind of music structure). At the beginning, there were only more than ten kinds of tunes, such as "Yang tune". With the development of the performance content and form, the music has been enriched and developed correspondingly. The first is to absorb some tunes from folk small tunes; The second is to borrow ideas from Bangzi Opera, Zhuizi Opera, Sizhou Opera and folk narrative-singing to create "gunbai" (recitation in the singing), "liaozi"(strating tune before singing) and "feiban"(free singing); The third is to use old tunes-making techniques called "jiqu" to create new tunes such as "Sibuxiang". At the same time, according to the needs of tune performance, this opera actively creates new tunes through learning the technique of "Banqiang Style" (a form of structural style in Chinese opera and quyi).

The performance of Northern Anhui Qu Opera is natural, simple and generous, with soft and melodious tunes. It has strong local characteristics and flavor, which is favored by the local people and serves as one of the most representative operas in the Huai River area. Its traditional repertoire has more than 200 plays, with a wide range of contents, most of which are based on historical records, legends and folk tales, expressing the local customs, people's living conditions, love and hatred stories, and aesthetic pursuits.

After nearly a hundred years of transmission, development and innovation, there were many talents appeared of Northern Anhui Qu Opera. They include artists such as Guo Lixian, Jiang Huachi, Du Xiaolin, Zhang Suzhi, Zhang Qingcai, Liu Cuihua, Zhang Shouhai, Cao Jinming, Wang Yuxia and Ge Xiaodong, directors such as Li Shengsan and Li Yitian, opera music theorists and composers such as Wang Qingzheng, playwrights such as Xu Tingsong, instrumentalists such as Liu Yunshan, conductors such as (drummer) Gu Yingbin, Quhu (a kind of stringing instrument) performers such as Liu Zhu and Liu Zhonghua. Among them, there is one of the top ten famous contemporary Chinese opera actors, Lu Ying. She is also an artist of Northern Anhui Qu Opera. These people have contributed a lot to the inheritance and development of Northern Anhui Qu Opera.

Fig 11 The Performing Pictures of Old Plays

In recent years, the Department of Culture of Fuyang city has attached great importance to the development of Northern Anhui Qu Opera with new operas created and more active performances. These works have won many awards in national, provincial and ministerial art performances: In 1989, the newly created Qing-dynasty-costume opera *Zheng Banqian Has Relatives by Marriage* won the first prize in the Second Provincial Art Festival, then performed in Beijing in 1990; In 1994, the newly created historical opera *Doctor Bianque and Emperor Qihuan* won the first prize in the Fourth Provincial Art Festival and provincial "excellent works in five aspects" award. In 1997, the newly created drama *Friends and Relatives* won the first prize in the Fifth Provincial Art Festival, provincial "excellent works in five aspects" award and Tian Han script award. In 2010, the modern opera *Wangjiaba* won the excellent script award in the Ninth Provincial Art Festival and provincial "excellent works in five aspects" award.

In November 2017, Northern Anhui Qu Opera entered the fifth list of province-level intangible cultural heritage representative items.

Three Traditional Folk Music

Huai River Gong-drum (province-level)

Huai River Gong-drum is an excellent folk art, which is widely spread in the Huai River basin with a long history.

Fig 12 Two Artists are Playing Gong-drum

The origin of Huai River Gong-drum is closely related to the war, which is legendary. According to the legend, the famous "Battle of the Fei River (383)" was happened at the foot of Bagong Mountain in Shou county of Huainan city. The Eastern Jin Dynasty (262-420) army and the Former Qin Empire (351-394) army confronted each other. They beat drums as a signal to attack and gongs to withdraw. The Jin army defeated the overwhelming Former Qin forces, and got a decisively victory through orderly advancing and retreating the troops with only minor casualties. In order to commemorate this famous battle, the local people often played gongs and drums along the Huai River, and gradually turned this custom into an art. During the Han Dynasty (202 BC-220 AD), gongs and drums entered the imperial court and became a part of "court music", then continued until now. After the appearance of Flower-drum Lanterns Dance, it quickly combined with dance and became a kind of accompaniment that was popular in Ming (1368-1644) and Qing (1636-1912) Dynasties.

In the cultures of Huai River, Huai River Gong-drum is a representative one, which has been popular along the river for a long time. It is a popular entertainment for the common people. Originated from the military music and rooted in the folk, Huai River Gong-drum developed in the entertainment life of the masses, then became a kind of Gong-drum music with strong local flavor. In the villages of Yingshang county, Huai River Gong-drum has a deep foundation. It has been passed down from generation to generation, which has been favored by people until now.

The development of Huai River Gong-drum is related to the local people's living habits and customs. The characteristics of enthusiasm, boldness and simplicity of Huai River Gong-drum fully reflect the characteristics of folk art of the Han nationality. This art reflects people's aspiration for the peace of the country and a good life. It also praises family harmony, social stability and people's living and working in peace and contentment with the display of Yingshang people's hardworking, wisdom, simpleness, kindness and indomitable spirit. There are many tunes, such as *Long Flowing Water* and *Eighteen Turns*. The method of performance is that the drum is used as conductor, the gong is used to play the main part and the bo and nao[①] are divided into two vocal parts for alternately beating. The performance is euphemistic and fluent sometimes, sonorous and powerful sometimes, and the points of gongs and drums are

---

① "bo and nao" refers to two kinds of copper percussion instrument with round shape.

varied. In the process of development, various places have formed their own artistic characteristics, such as awe-inspiring Gong-drum in Lukou town, Gong-drum in sheds in Xinji town and Huagu opera Gong-drum in Shencheng town, which are all representative.

In recent years, many good works of Huai River Gong-drum have emerged, such as *Long Flowing Water*, *Eighteen Turns*, *Small Ten Points*, *Five Gong-beaters*, *Small Five Turns*, *The Rabbit Digs Its Burrow*, *Opening Performance of Gong-drums*. The performances are also unprecedentedly active, with more than 20 folk performance groups and more than 700 performing artists. Each year, more than 100 performances are performed in Fuyang city, Huainan city, Fengtai county and Shou county, etc., which are well-received.

In December 2008, Huai River Gong-drum entered the second list of province-level intangible cultural heritage representative items.

Fentai Suona (province-level)

Fentai Suona has a history of more than 600 years. It comes from the folk of Taihe county with a broad mass base.

According to *History of Chinese Music*, the schools of suona in Anhui province can be divided into Southern Anhui school and Northern Anhui school. In Northern Anhui school, there are two representative branches. One branch is located at Yangshan village and Su county in Northeast Anhui, and the other is located at Fuyang city, Taihe county and Bozhou city. Fengtai town of Taihe county is located at the Northwest Anhui, which is adjacent to Henan province and Shandong province. In the process of spreading, it absorbed the elements of popular operas, such as Bangzi Opera, Zhuizi Opera, Qingyin (a kind of Chinese quyi), Qu Opera, Sizhou Opera and folk arts and small tunes. Then it gradually formed its own artistic characteristics, serving as one of the main representative schools of suona in Anhui province.

Fig 13 The Picture of Playing Suona

As a leading instrument, suona is often performed with gongs and drums. The performance of Fentai Suona is full of enthusiasm and magnificent atmosphere. It is especially suitable for playing bold and fierce tunes, which can deeply and delicately express inner thoughts and feelings. In the performance of the plays, it not only retains the traditional skills such as single tonguing, double tonguing and portamento. At the same time, according to the needs of performing, it created many difficult skills, such as super high tonguing, borrowed tonguing, air haunch-up tonguing, air top tonguing, three-string tonguing, flute tonguing and oboe tonguing. It can also imitate the crowing of chickens and birds, singing of people (commonly known as Kazi Opera), so as to improve its artistic expression.

Originated from the folk, Fentai Suona has strong vitality. It is an indispensable form of folk activities and mass cultural entertainment to render the atmosphere. In Fentai town and its surrounding areas, there is a custom of inviting the suona troupe to play tunes at weddings, funerals, temple fairs and sacrificial activities. Its main plays include *Big Flute Stirring, Dragon King, Calling Xunzi, Scratching Books*; Its blowing plays mainly include *Lady General Mu Takes Command, Taming of The Princess, Dividing Son, Li Suping, Rolling Mat Tube*. Its main plays of Sizhou Opera include *Picking Cotton, Drinking Noodle Soup, Zhuge Liang Condoling*, etc. The number of these plays has more about 100.

In recent years, the plays performed by artists of Fentai Suona have won many awards in province and municipal art activities. The reporter of CCTV once interviewed folk suona artists in Fentai town and made special report. In the history of folk music in Anhui province, because of the position held by the suona, Fentai town is known as "the hometown of Suona".

In November 2017, Fentai Suona entered the fifth list of province-level intangible cultural heritage representative items.

Four Traditional Sports, Entertainment and Aerobatics

Linquan Aerobatics (province-level)

Linquan Acrobatics has a long history. In the 1950s, a number of cultural relics were unearthed in Linquan county which include the pottery theater of the Western Han Dynasty (202 BC-8 AD) and colored acrobatic figurines. Archaeologists inferred that acrobatics has existed in Linquan county for about 2000 years. In the middle of Ming Dynasty (1400-1580), some programs were performed by the aerobatics troupe (stage name: Yizuomao) in Linquan county, such as "guohe daoshan" (similar to "walking on the tightrope"). These programs had a far-reaching influence in the folk.

Acrobatics, known as "baixi[1]" in ancient times, belongs to shanyue[2], which was developed in the Western Zhou Dynasty (1046 BC-771 BC) and flourished in the Han Dynasty (202 BC-220 AD). Located at the junction site of Chinese northern and southern cultures, Linquan county has simple folk custom and strong martial atmosphere since ancient times. Thus, people here especially admire acrobatic circus. For those who are living at the grass-roots level took activities of acrobatic circus to support their families. One family is a unit of circus troupes, which features the early form of Linquan Acrobatics teams.

In the new era, Linquan Acrobatics has developed rapidly, forming a number of professional acrobatic towns, villages and households. Weixiao village, located in Weizhai town, Linquan county, was branded as

---

① "baixi" refers to the general term for folk performing arts in ancient China.

② "shanyue" refers to the combination of baixi and acrobatics.

"professional acrobatics village". Some circuses, such as Yingxian Circus, Feiyan Acrobatic Troupe, Yingxian Youth Acrobatic Troupe and Monkey King Circus came to prominence. The actors have taken part in films such as *Love and Hatred of Red Revenge*, *The Great Xiangguo Temple* and *The Soul of Art*. At present, there are 872 teams with cultural performance licenses in Linquan county, with more than 20000 employees. The annual income of acrobatics industry is more than 500 million yuan, which has become an important part of local economic development.

Fig 14 Old Picture of Linquan Aerobatics

Based on current situations, the local cultural authorities adopted measures to promote the steady development of Linquan Acrobatics. A number of new and ingenious programs created by themselves were well-received by the audience. From 2009 to 2017, Culture Department of Anhui province successfully held four "Folk Acrobatic Art Festivals" in Linquan county, with an audience of 300000; The large-scale magic show *Magic Love* won the gold award in the Third "Golden Cane Award" Magic Conference in the Yangtze River Delta region; In 2014, Hu Jun and his daughter Hu Siyuan got well-received in CCTV's program, *Brilliant Chinese* through their work *Rope Skills*. Hu Siyuan was honored as one of the "top ten actors in Anhui province "; In 2016, the first acrobatic film *The Soul of Art* was released in China. With deep international cultural exchanges, Linquan Acrobatics has also gone abroad, and has been invited to the United States, Sweden, Egypt, Thailand and other countries to carry out cultural exchange activities. Therefore, Linquan county has won the honorary titles of "the hometown of Chinese folk culture and art", "the hometown of Chinese acrobatics" and "national advanced cultural unit". At present, Linquan Acrobatics is preparing to enter the fifth list of state-level intangible cultural heritage representative items.

In December 2006, Linquan Aerobatics entered the first list of province-level intangible cultural heritage representative items.

Tongcheng Fire Fork and Fire Whip (province-level)

Originated from the Warring States Period (475 BC-221 BC), Tongcheng Fire Fork and Fire Whip has a long history. In the early stage, fire fork and fire whip were mainly used to fight or deter invaders, and gradually turned into a performance in sacrificial activities in the late Ming and early Qing Dynasty period (1600-1644). This kind of performance ceremony has been handed down from generation to generation and also has become an important part of Linquan folk culture.

Tongcheng, an ancient town in the Northern Anhui, formerly known as Tongyang, is under the jurisdiction of Linquan county. The Chinese character " 銅 " (Tong) is a special word for naming a place in the dictionary. As early as the Han Dynasty (202 BC-220 AD), there was Tongyang county in Tongcheng. In the first year of Yongchu period of Southern Dynasty (420), Liu Yu set a new county here which was named as "Beixin Caijun" (means a northern new county). In the late Ming and early Qing Dynasty period (1600-1644), Tongcheng had developed into one of the four important towns in the western Fuyang and became local economical, cultural, technological and educational center. Tongcheng has an important geographical location with strong folk customs and popular martial atmosphere.

Fork, was originally a production tool for fishing and hunting in ancient times, then evolved into a weapon. Whip, earlier than fork, was also one of the ancient weapons in China and is widely used in the Spring and Autumn Period (770 BC-476 BC) and Warring States Period (475 BC-221 BC). Fire fork and fire whip are fire attacking weapons invented by the ancients based on fork and whip. It was said that fire fork and fire whip, as important weapons, were introduced into Tongcheng by Li

Zicheng[①]. After the failure of the uprising, the general became a traveling monk and came to Tongcheng to beg. He turned the fire fork and fire whip into the equipment of martial arts performance in exchange for food.

Fig 15 An Old Artist is Playing Fire Fork and Fire Whip

Local acrobatic and sports enthusiasts followed the traveling monk to learn and mproved this performance after mastering its skills. Late, it become a traditional festival performance and a way to keep fit. After hundreds of years of transmission and development, Tongcheng Fire Fork and Fire Whip has made bold improvement and innovation based on traditional martial arts stance, gait and techniques. It integrated the gait and technique of Yangko Dance, absorbed more elements of folk acrobatics and martial arts, forming a unique performancc form of acrobatics and competition. It is widely spread and well-received. In the 1970s, Ma Enyun, a famous artist of Tongcheng Fire Fork and Fire Whip, sat up the "Eastern Tongcheng Houchengzi Art Troupe". The troupe developed from 20 people at the beginning to more than 100 people now,

---

① "Li Zicheng" is a leader of an uprising army which is made of farmers to overthrow Ming Dynasty and establish a new regime.

playing the role of transmission, development and innovation of this art. From 2009 to 2017, Tongcheng Fire Fork and Fire Whip had participated in the performances of the opening ceremony of the Fourth Province Folk Acrobatics Festival and other important provincial and municipal festival activities.

In July 2010, Tongcheng Fire Fork and Fire Whip entered the third list of province-level intangible cultural heritage representative items.

Wuyin Bagua[①] Boxing (province-level)

Wuyin Bagua Boxing is a kind of Chinese boxing of Han nationality. It is developed based on "Fu Xi Bagua Boxing", which is mainly spread among the people in Funan county of Anhui province.

Liu Huai, founder of Fu Xi Bagua Boxing, courtesy name Daoyuan (Chinese: 道元), art name Nanmu Laoren (Chinese: 南木老人), was born in the Qianlong reign (1736-1796) of Qing Dynasty. Luo Tixian, the first heritor of Liu Huai, deeply inherited the essence of Fu Xi Bagua Boxing. After finishing apprenticeship, he traveled many famous mountains and rivers and made friends with his kung-fu. He visited many kung-fu schools such as Wudang, Shaolin and E'mei, absorbed their strengths and essence. After a long period of thinking and physical understanding, according to the thought of dynamic relationship between Yin and Yang[②] and Wuxing[③], he created a brand-new school of martial arts which was named as Wuyin Bagua Boxing. Its characteristics are paying attention to practice with flexible routines, various forms, comprehensive techniques, unique styles.

---

① "Bagua" are eight symbols used in Taoist cosmology to represent the fundamental principles of reality, seen as a range of eight interrelated concepts.

② "Yin and Yang" is a concept of dualism in ancient Chinese philosophy, describing how seemingly opposite or contrary forces may actually be complementary, interconnected, and interdependent in the natural world, and how they may give rise to each other as they interrelate to one another.

③ "Wuxing" is a fivefold conceptual scheme that many traditional Chinese fields used to explain a wide array of phenomena, from cosmic cycles to the interaction between internal organs, and from the succession of political regimes to the properties of medicinal drugs. It is usually translated as Five Phases which include Fire, Water, Wood, Gold and Soil.

It also pays attention to the practice of Qi[①] and strength with inside and outside cultivation.

Fig 16 The Gesture of Wuyin Bagua Boxing

Wuyin Bagua Boxing of Funan county was inherited by Fang Ruichen, a native of Funan county in the early years of the Republic of China (1912-1949). He absorbed various elements of folk martial arts in Funan area and carried out transmission, improvement and development. Ma jusen and Li Yuming, the sixth-generation heritors, carried forward this boxing, and spread it to Fuyang city, Linquan county, Bozhou city and other places in Northwest Anhui, with many learners and far-reaching influence.

In May 2014, Wuyin Bagua Boxing entered the fourth list of province-level intangible cultural heritage representative items.

---

① "Qi" is the basic element that constitute the cosmos and, through its movements, changes and transformations, produces everything in the world, including the human body and life activities. In the field of medicine, qi refers both to the refined nutritive substance that flows within the human body as well as to its functional activities.

Taihe Wudang[①] Tai Chi[②] (province-level)

Taihe Wudang Tai Chi is a branch of Tai chi which is directly inherited from Taoism. It dosen't have direct relationship with the current Tai chi schools. It is a relatively independent school of martial arts.

Since Tai chi was introduced into the folk from Taoism, there has been many schools named by surnames of its founder. In line with social popular naming, it is also called Taihe Wudang Tai Chi. Taihe Wudang Tai Chi, also known as "Yihe Tai Chi", has been popular in Taihe county for a long time. In addition, this boxing comes from Wudang school, and its founder is Zhang Sanfeng[③]. Thus, it was named from its founder. The founder, Zhang Sanfeng, created the essence of Tai chi, the method of health preservation and body protection, which was passed down to Zhang Gushan, the second-generation heritor, and then Liu Guquan and Qiu Yuanjing, the third generation. Later, it has been passed down from generation to generation until now for 14 generations.

The cultivating method of Taihe Wudang Tai Chi integrates physical and consciousness training. In terms of theory and techniques in boxing and kung-fu, it has great differences with other popular schools of Tai chi. It has three training steps: softening tendon, softening bone and softening marrow; It has five types of training methods: sitting, standing, walking, moving and using; Besides, there are ten post-training methods combined

---

① "Wudang" here refers to a school of Chinese Kung-fu.

② "Tai Chi", sometimes colloquially known as "Shadowboxing", is an internal Chinese martial art practiced for defense training, health benefits, and meditation.

③ "Zhang Sanfeng" was a legendary Chinese Taoist who invented Tai chi and was purported to have achieved immortality.

with internal and external wuxing① which are essence, spirit, consciousness, pneuma, power, tendon, bone, skin, hair and muscle.

Fig 17 The Gesture of Taihe Wudang Tai Chi

Because of the secret transmission of Taoism, there are strict regulations on this. One generation must hold Tai chi for sixty years, and within the 60 years, there can't be more than two people accepting the transmission. Therefore, Taihe Wudang Tai Chi is rarely spread among the people, and it is on the verge of being lost and needs to be rescued.

In November 2017, Taihe Wudang Tai Chi entered the fifth list of province-level intangible cultural heritage representative items.

---

① "wuxing" is a fivefold conceptual scheme that many traditional Chinese fields used to explain a wide array of phenomena, from cosmic cycles to the interaction between internal organs, and from the succession of political regimes to the properties of medicinal drugs. It is usually translated as Five Phases which include Fire, Water, Wood, Gold and Soil.

Five Traditional Dance

Yingshang Flower-drum Lantern Dance (state-level)

Flower-drum Lantern Dance is an outstanding folk art with distinctive features in Anhui province. It is an art form combining singing and dancing, which is widely spread in the Huai River basin with plenty of participants and great influence. It is one of the typical representatives of Chinese dances, combining dance, gong-drum music, singing and scene opera. The name of flower-drum lantern comes from the fact that the early performance was mostly performed on the flat open land in the countryside at night, such as the wheat field (or the rice field) and under the illumination of flower lanterns.

The performance of Flower-drum Lantern Dance has a long history in the Huai River basin. By the end of 1930s and 40s, it spread to more than 20 counties and cities of Anhui province, Henan province, Shandong province and Jiangsu province with the center of Bengbu city, Fuyang city and Huainan city in Anhui province. It is one of people's favorite entertainment forms along the Huai River. Yingshang county is one of the three main birthplaces of Flower-drum Lantern Dance in the Huai River basin. Chang Renxia, a master of modern oriental aesthetics, was born in Yingshang county. There is a description in his book *History of Chinese Dances* that the history of Flower-drum Lantern Dance can be traced back to 500 years ago. According to this description, Yingshang Flower-drum Lantern Dance originated in the early Ming Dynasty and took shape in the Kangxi reign (1622-1722) and Qianlong reign (1736-1795) of the Qing Dynasty. During the Daoguang reign (1821-1850) of Qing Dynasty, "big flower scene", also called as "lantern dancing" and "performing red lanterns" by the local people, was its predecessor. In the early years of the Republic of China, this kind performance of folk dance became popular in rural areas of Yingshang county. Many performance teams had emerged, forming a situation of "thousands of gongs and drums, thousands of lanterns dances troupes" and lasting performance activities.

In 1921, Tang Peijin, a folk artist, made a historic reform of the traditional Flower-drum Lantern Dance in remote Huangwa village of Yingshang county. He absorbed various opera tunes, coupled with diverse orchestral instruments, and created two unique tunes called "Dayouchang" and "Xiaoyouchang", thus, forming the distinctive artistic style of Yingshang Flower-drum Lantern Dance. Tang Peijin organized a troupe with a large lineup to go out to perform. Everywhere he went, there were thousands of people and his performance was well-received. Artists from Fengtai county, Funan county, Huoqiu county and other places along the Huai River also came to acknowledge him as their master. Yingshang Flower-drum Lantern Dance gained a great reputation and quickly spread at that time.

Yingshang county is known as "the hometown of Guan Zhong[1], the water-town of Northern Anhui province". It has been a beautiful place with outstanding personages since ancient times. Flower-drum Lantern Dance is one of the well-preserved original folk arts. In terms of the resources, Yingshang Flower-drum Lantern Dance was created from labors, and gradually matured after the painstaking processing, sorting, creation and modification of artists. In terms of content, it enlarged to a

---

① "Guan Zhong" was a Chinese philosopher and politician. He served as chancellor and was a reformer of the State of Qi during the Spring and Autumn Period of Chinese history.

comprehensive dance art with dance as the main part, accompanied by a variety of musical instruments, singing and opera from the earliest single lantern dance. In terms of performance form, handsome men (nickname: "drum shelf") and beautiful women (nickname: "orchid") are singing and dancing together. The performance is characterized by vigorous, simple cheerful, warm, free and easy dance movements with rich local flavor. The music is derived from folk songs with varied rhythms which are high and exciting or gentle and delicate. The instrument is a kind of folk percussion instrument, with distinct rhythm. People are playing and dancing at the same time, which is very expressive. The opera has wonderful melody, which has not only the vigor and simplicity of songs and dances in Northern China, but also the flexibility and beauty of song and dances in Southern China.

Fig 18 Group Performance of Yingshang Flower-drum Lantern Dance

The structure of Yingshang Flower-drum Lantern Dance is relatively complete, which is composed of dance, singing, gong-drum orchestral accompaniment and small opera performance of the end part. The scene (stage) can be small or large. The small flower scene (includes two-person dance, three-person dance or four-person dance) offers a relaxed and elegant feeling to the audience. The big flower scene (group dance) is lively, magnificent, elegant and extraordinary. Originated from the folk, Yingshang Flower-drum Lantern Dance has not only the simpleness and earthy fragrance of the countryside, but also the water charm of the Huai River. The dance moves are simple with strong beat, such as "douboji" (imitating the gait when people are shaking dustpan), "danlaolan" (imitating the gait when people are salvaging basket), "duanzhenbian" (imitating the gait when people are holding plaque), "yongzibu"(imitating moves of a pupae), "ba'nibu"(imitating the gait when people are trying to pull foot out of mud) and shangsanbu (imitating the gait when people are going uphill). These moves are mostly refined and developed from agricultural production and daily life. The performance is cordial and natural to watch, which is deeply loved by local people. Especially in the performance, the artists flexibly use handkerchief and towel as props, accompanied by beautiful dance and sonorous accompaniment, which looks like a graceful fairy scattering flowers, leaving a deep and beautiful impression on the audience.

Since the reform and opening up, Yingshang Flower-drum Lantern Dance has got great protection and transmission under the attention of the Party and the government. Wang Chuanxian (stage name: yitiaosheng) and Huang Xicheng (stage name: huanghouzi) were titled as "top ten veteran artists of Flower-drum Lantern Dance in Anhui province". Especially after the establishment of Art Troupe of Yingshang Flower-drum Lantern Dance in 2009, it has made great achievements. The play *Bass Drum and Small Orchid* participated in the National Traditional Dance Competition held at China Intangible Cultural Heritage Protection Center in Hangzhou in 2009 and won the gold medal in the competition; In 2010, the play, *Joyful Songs of Huai River* participated in the Tenth China Art Festival and won the highest award of national mass culture and art, the galaxy award; In 2012, the play, *Coming to Flower-drum Village in Spring* participated in the Ninth China Folk Art Festival and won the gold medal; In 2017, the play, *Dreaming Flower-drum Lantern Dance* participated in the performance with the theme of "Celebration of the Twentieth Anniversary of Hong Kong's Return" and won the gold medal; In 2019, on behalf of China, this dance participated in the Youth International Art Festival held in Singapore and won the special award. It also participated in the National Farmers' Song Festival, Provincal Folk Culture Festival, Acrobatics Festival and other mass cultural activities, and was interviewed and reported by CCTV and other media.

In May 2006, Yingshang Flower-drum Lantern Dance entered the first list of state-level intangible cultural heritage representative items.

Taihe Lion Lantern Dance (province-level)

Taihe Lion Lantern Dance has a history of more than 100 years. It integrates martial arts, acrobatics, athletics, totem and entertainment. It is a unique form of folk dance.

Zhang Shouben, the founder of Taihe Lion Lantern Dance, was born in 1849. He has been practicing martial arts since he was a child. He also has excellent kung fu. He likes to gather a group of martial arts fans on traditional festivals such as the Dragon Boat Festival, Mid-Autumn Festival and Spring Festival, uses the self-made "lion" as props to entertain himself and celebrates the festival. He invented simple and primitive dance moves, mostly expressing the lion's pleasure, anger, sorrow and joy. These moves became the predecessor of today's "Taihe Lion Lantern Dance". This kind of dance has been handed down and widely spread in today's society.

Fig 19 Street Performance of Lion Lantern Dance

The lion lantern is made of bamboo, wood and colored stripes. In general, the lion dance is performed in pairs with one person wearing an old colorful costume acting as a training "warrior" who fights and plays with the "lion". The lion and the warrior cooperate with tacit understanding. This dance is mainly performed in festivals to express people's happy mood and good wishes, accompanied by sympathetic gongs and drums, high-pitched suona and other musical instruments. The performance is grand, lively and festive with full of routines. The general procedures are the follows. The training "warrior" will lead the lion into the arena with a ball at first. Then the "lion" performer displays lion's running, jumping, skipping, rolling, pouncing, standing, lying and turning in order to imitate real lion's strong power, anger state, shaking head and tail, etc. In addition, the "lion" can also jump on the table and perform such breathtaking actions as rolling embroidered ball, walking the rope at high altitude, walking tall and slender stakes. At the same time, the fireworks add a lively atmosphere. The whole performance is thrilling and interesting with many climaxes, which is very popular among the masses.

During the Anti-Japanese War, Zhang Tianrong, the son of Zhang Shouben and the heritor of Taihe Lion Lantern Dance, gathered martial arts lovers in Dongguan village to rehearse the lion lantern dance. The performances of Dongguan Lion Lantern Dance became popular because of the solid martial arts skills of the dancers and their superb performing ability. During the Spring Festival, the team will perform to enjoy themselves with local people. The large-scale performances mainly included the performance to celebrate the victory of the Anti-Japanese war in 1945, the performance to welcome the people's liberation army of China in 1949, and the performance to celebrate the tenth anniversary of the founding of New China in 1959. These performances had produced extraordinary effects.

Hongshan Acrobatic Troupe, which was established in 1956, inherited and developed Taihe Lion Lantern Dance. They not only put on the lion lantern dance as a reserved program, but also added more wonderful contents, such as the lion drilling fire circle and walking on the seesaw. The troupe was well-received, and the spreading areas expanded rapidly. The troupe had performed in Bozhou city, Jieshou city, Fuyang city of Anhui province and some counties in Henan province.

In recent years, under the government's attention on folk art, Zhao Jihu, the fifth-generation heritor of Taihe Lion Lantern Dance, founded the "Dragon and Lion Dance Club" which recruited more than 30 young people with martial arts skills to train the lion dance, making this wonderful folk dance art bloom again.

In December 2008, Taihe Lion Lantern Dance entered the second list of province-level intangible cultural heritage representative items.

Red Lantern Dance (province-level)

Red Lantern Dance is a kind of folk dance with local characteristics. This dance has been popular for a long time in Funan county.

According to the words of the old artists from generation to generation, Red Lantern dancers regarded Li Shimin, emperor Taizong (598-649) of Tang Dynasty, as the master. It was said that Li Shimin's army was defeated in the war. They retreated to the small town on the south bank of the Gu River and were besieged by the enemy. Li Shimin adopted the advice of the strategists and local people, used the opportunity of performing lantern dance to "mix" into the masses, then went out of the town. On that day, he and the soldiers put on the local festival costumes, and Li Shimin played as the "umbrella handler" of Red Lantern Dance with other soldiers as supporting roles. They beat the gong-drums, performed the Red Lantern Dance, swaggered out of the city, and successfully escaped from the siege of the enemy.

Later, Li Shimin became the emperor of the Tang Dynasty. He was awarded the person who playing the "umbrella handle" as "master of lantern". From then on, Funan Red Lantern Dance was no longer treated as insignificant art. Instead, it was treated as "the superior art". The used "red lantern umbrella" was put into the hall "to be respected", and the artists could also sit in the hall to eat. In the old society, ordinary "artists" did not have such treatment. This is the reason why the artists of "Red Lantern Dance" in Funan county always regard Lin Shimin as their "master".

The Red Lantern Dance generally consists of nine people. The one who hold the "umbrella handle" as the protagonist, commands the team to change formation and masters the rhythm. The role of surrounding four people is female in general, acting as wax flower to decorate the "umbrella handle". They hold handkerchiefs in their left hand and colorful fans in their right hand, dancing with the sonorous gongs and drums; The following two who carry drums are clowns. They carry drums on their backs and drumsticks in both hands, drumming while dancing.

Fig 20 Rural Performance of Red Lantern Dance

The performance of Red Lantern Dance is simple and natural with humorous singing. In the accompaniment of gongs and drums, the actors dance with the rhythm. As soon as the gongs and drums stop, they begin to perform impromptu, or singing freely without routines, or expressing their aspirations with objects and feelings with scenery, which has a strong local flavor. In 1990, on behalf of Funan county, the team of "Red Lantern Dance" participated in the First Province Flower-drum Lantern Dance Festival held in Bengbu city and won the silver award.

In 2007, the Party Committee and government of Funan county started to protect this rare cultural heritage by funding and arranging special personnel which is responsible for excavation and inheritance. Combined with the efforts of many artists, remarkable results have been achieved. At present, Red Lantern Dance teams of Taoyuan village and other places are still active in urban and rural areas of Funan county.

In November 2017, Red Lantern Dance entered the fifth list of province-level intangible cultural heritage representative items.

Six Traditional Craftsmanship

Jieshou Painted Pottery (state-level)

Jieshou Painted Pottery, also known as tricolor carved pottery, was first found in the folk kiln site of the Tang Dynasty (618-907). Its production techniques adhere to the style of "Tang Tri-Color Glazed Ceramics" and absorbe the artistic style of paper-cut and woodblock printing from the Central Plains. It has a long history with its own style. In 1999, one of the top ten archaeological discoveries in China, the ancient canal archaeological discoveries of Liuzi village of Huaibei city, unearthed many pieces of Jieshou tri-color pottery. The UK's Victoria Museum also collect Jieshou tri-color carved pottery.

The legend about the birth of Jieshou Painted Pottery is complicated. But the birth of each dynamic art is related to the local natural conditions and people's yearning for a better life. Shaying River is the largest tributary of Huai River and runs through Jieshou city. Local people call Shaying River as Sha River. Since the Song Dynasty (960-1279), the Yellow River had burst many times and flooded southward into the Huai River. Sha River, located in the hinterland of the Central Plains, was the first to bear the brunt. This not only brought disaster to the people, but also brought a kind of high viscous "clay" formed by a large amount of sediment deposition. This kind of clay is just a good raw material for firing pottery. Among the residents on both sides of Sha River, it has been a custom to give pottery altars and bottles as dowry to their daughters when their daughters get married. These pottery altars and bottles are carved with auspicious patterns with the theme of plum, orchid, bamboo, chrysanthemum, insect, fish, bird and beast. Pottery can be used as household utensils as well as the blessing of their mother's family. This custom virtually promoted the birth of painted pottery and the improvement of its techniques.

According to the records, there were famous "Jieshou thirteen kilns" on the south bank of Sha River in the Ming (1368-1644) and Qing (1636-1912) Dynasties. The thirteen villages were all engaged in pottery making and were named as "pottery kilns", such as Lu kiln, Wei kiln, Zhu kiln, Yin kiln, Zhang kiln, Tian kiln, Wang kiln. At that time, the kiln continued for several miles with billowing smoke, forming a magnificent scene. It was the heyday of the production of Jieshou Painted Pottery in history. In the long course of development, craftsmen learned from each other, absorbed strengths of other folk arts to improve their craft. The outstanding achievement was the appearance of an engraving and production technique called "daomaren" which gradually became the main technique to create pottery. After the appreance of this technique, the shape of pottery became more plump and mellow, thick and simple, with obvious characteristics of the Central Plains. In terms of carving design, the themes were more and more broad. Historical stories and opera characters were also engraved on the pottery. The engraving techniques became more and more perfect, and the brushwork became more and more delicate and lifelike. After firing, the characters and animal patterns on the pottery were vivid with high artistic value. The painted pottery embodied the characters of farmers in Northern China and their aesthetic taste. It also reflected the aesthetic orientation of China's folk art for advocating nature and pursuing harmony, serving as the essence of the folk art of Central Plains.

Lu Shanyi, a veteran artist of Jieshou city, is a representative personage who contributed a lot in the development history of painted pottery. He absorbed the creative technique of "daomaren" which was created and improved in Tang Dynasty (618-907), Song Dynasty (960-1279), Ming Dynasty (1368-1644), Qing Dynasty (1636-1912), and the Republic of China (1912-1949), then made great innovations. In terms of the production process, theme selection and color application of painted pottery, Lu's works tends to be simple, rough and deep. In order to meet these changes, Lu Shanyi decorates the tread with two layers of make-up soil[①], thus showing two basic contrast colors of ochre and yellow or ochre and white in the process of dyeing. In terms of engraving themes, besides using flowers, birds, fish and insects as creation objects, it also focuses on absorbing artistic elements from traditional dramas and expressing them in the form of scenes, which makes the quality of Jieshou Painted Pottery to a new level. Lushanyi's "daomaren" series works have become the representative works of Jieshou Painted Pottery and he also got the title of "master of Chinese folk arts and crafts" in 2006.

In the new era, Jieshou Painted Pottery develops rapidly. A group of professionals are emerging who are interested in the development of painted pottery. There are also many companies engaged in the development of painted pottery with Wang Jingsheng Painted Pottery Art Co., Ltd., Lu Style Carved Painted Pottery Co., Ltd. and Lihua Painted Pottery Studio as the representatives. In recent years, Jieshou Painted Pottery has participated in large-scale exhibitions at home and abroad, such as the First Folk Culture Festival in Anhui province, the Third Chinese National Art Treasures Culture Festival, the Sixth China International Hui Merchants Conference, Anhui Week of World

---

① "make-up soil" refers to a kind of thin layer of color paste left on the surface of the pottery.

Exposition, the Fifth China Folk Arts and Crafts Exposition, the Eleventh Masters' Works of Chinese Arts and Crafts and International Art Exposition, Macao Spring Festival Folk Custom Exposition in 2011, and the Cross-strait Arts and Crafts Exposition. The works of Jieshou Painted Pottery have won many awards and been collected by many museums.

Fig 21 The Collection of Painted Potteries

In May 2006, Jieshou Painted Pottery entered the first list of state-level intangible cultural heritage representative items.

Linquan Brush (province-level)

Linquan Brush got its name because it is produced in Tanpeng town of Linquan county. It has a long history. In ancient times, it was called "Meng brush". It was said that the earliest brush was made by general Meng Tian of Qin Dynasty (221 BC-207 BC). In Tanpeng town, there are relics of the military temple of general Meng Tian. Local people worship him in the relics and regard him as the "founder of brush".

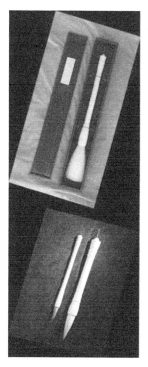

Fig 22 The Display of Linquan Brush

In the late Ming Dynasty (1567-1611), "Yuansheng Brush Shop" was established in the west of Tanpeng town, which showed that brush making had a large scale at that time. People also called the brush as "Ming brush". During the Xianfeng reign (1851-1862) of the Qing Dynasty, Li Wanzhong, a brush maker in the eastern Tanpeng town, founded the

"Mingdaotang Brush Shop". The name of this shop adopted the meaning of "inheriting the techniques of predecessors in Ming Dynasty and making a good pen". Xu Guangjin, a famous official and calligrapher of Fuyang in the Qing Dynasty (1636-1912), once praised Linquan Brush that "the brush made by Mingdaotang has the best quality among the brushes."

Linquan county is near the beautiful Quan River, so the name of the county comes from its location. It was called "Qinqiu" in ancient times with a civilization history of more than 3000 years. During the Spring and Autumn Period (475 BC-221 BC), there was Shenzi State which was the fief of Ran Jizai, the tenth son of Emperor Wen of Zhou Dynasty (about 1152 BC-1056 BC). Linquan also is the hometown of Jiang Shang[1], a famous historical and cultural figure. Xia Culture[2], Central Plains Culture, Huai-Yi Culture[3], and Chu Culture integrated in this area, forming a profound historical accumulation. Since ancient times, the style of writing has been flourished. There is a tradition of farming, reading, calligraphy and painting among local people. As an industry, brush making has emerged and has been growing.

The techniques of Linquan Brush follow the characteristics of traditional hand-made techniques. By using local wool, weasel hair (from winter to the beginning of spring of the second year), wolf tail, bristle, rabbit hair from south of the Huai River and local hemp as raw materials,

---

① "Jiang Shang" was a Chinese noble who helped kings Wen and Wu of Zhou Dynasty (about 1046 BC– 256 BC) overthrow the Shang Dynasty (about 1600 BC–1046 BC) in ancient China.

② "Xia Culture" refers to the material and cultural remains left by the residents of Xia Dynasty (about 2070 BC–1600 BC)

③ "Huai–Yi Culture" refers to the material and cultural remains left by an ancient tribe living in Huai River and Yellow River of Shang (about 1600 BC–1046 BC) and Zhou (about 1046 BC– 256 BC) Dynasties.

Linquan Brush goes through more than 100 processes, such as picking hair, soaking hair, making brush head, adding hemp lining, kneading brush head, making brush holder and stuffing brush head. Then after repeated elaborate combing, bundling, bucket loading, brush repairing and other processes, the brush is formed. With exquisite craftsmanship and excellent production, Linquan Brush has been loved and well-known by literati since its birth.

The main producing area of Linquan Brush is Tanpeng town. There are many brush making companies such as "Lintan Brush Shop", "Wendetang" and "Mingdaotang". Their products are famous for "Tan brush". With the characteristics of advanced techniques, pure and durable hair, and the combination of hardness and softness, Tan brush is well-known in the industry of calligraphy and painting, and has been rated as a national excellent product. During the 14th National Congress of the Communist Party of China in 1992, an elaborate Jiulong brush was presented to Comrade Deng Xiaoping as a precious gift by the Anhui delegation. This brush is now in the National Museum of China. In the spring of 1995, Comrade Hua Guofeng wrote down two Chinese character "Guo Bao" (Chinese character: 国宝, which means "national treasure") with great interest by using "Tan brush". Now, this brush is collected in Wendetang Brush Shop in Linquan county. At the same time, Linquan Brush also served as presents to the first chief executive of Hong Kong, Tung Chee Hwa, and the visiting leaders of relevant countries and regions. Linquan Brush was widely welcomed, leaving good memory.

Since the new era, Linquan Brush has been developing and innovating. Because of its exquisite workmanship and excellent quality, it occupies an important position in the national pen making industry. It has won many honors such as "Hundred Flowers Award" of the National Arts and Crafts. It has a number of invention patents, and has a certificate of inspection exemption. The products have been exported to more than ten countries and regions, such as Japan, Southeast Asia and Western Europe. Therefore, Linquan county is also known as the "hometown of brush in Northern China". Shen Peng, a famous calligrapher and former chairman of China Calligraphers Association, once praised that using Tan brush like "dragon flies and tiger goes with the wind, then the city is cold"(which means "lively and vigorous flourishes in calligraphy"). Sun Mofo, an veteran calligrapher, inscribed it with the four Chinese characters of "Guifutiangong"(Chinese character: 神工鬼斧, which means "prodigious skill"). Fan Zeng, a famous calligrapher and painter, praised it as a "treasure of the study". Zhao Puchu, Qi Gong, Wu Zuoren, Han Meilin, Liu Zishan, Mu Xiaotian, Gu Meiqin, and Tao Tianyue also inscribed, wrote poems, and painted respectively to sincerely praise Tan brush.

In December 2008, Linquan Brush entered the second list of province-level intangible cultural heritage representative items.

Wenwang Gong Liquor Brewing (province-level)

The brewing techniques of Wenwang Gong Liquor have been handed down for thousands of years. According to the *Records of the Historian*, the fief of Ran Jizai, the tenth son of Emperor Wen of Zhou Dynasty (about 1152 BC-1056 BC) is located at Linquan county. At that time, the local fertile plain was rich in grain so that liquor workshops were all over the countryside. Gradually, there was a liquor brewing method made by five cereals formed, that was, using wheat, millet, bean and other cereals to mix, cook and dry, then added with distiller's yeast and placed them in the pottery jar, with the mouth of the jar sealing with mud and straw covering on the jar to ferment. Finally, the fragrant liquor will form after more than ten days.

Fig 23 The Brewing Processes of Wenwang Gong Liquor

In the brewing processes of Wenwang Gong Liquor, the brewing technique of "Shen-style Special Liquor" has the greatest influence on it. "Shen-style Special Liquor" was made by Shen family, a local gentleman in Linquan county in the Song Dynasty (960-1279). This liquor was fermented with five kinds of cereals of soybean, rice, sorghum, glutinous rice and wheat. It is said that Su Shi[①], a great poet who was once the governor of Yingzhou district, tasted this kind of liquor and wrote a good sentence of "liquor makes beauty's skin pale red". In the early Ming Dynasty (1368-1435), Wang family inherited Shen's liquor workshops and summed up "Wang-style secret recipe". Therefore, this liquor had two names, scholars called it "Shen-style Special Liquor", while the common people called it "miscellaneous cereal liquor", which is the predecessor of Wenwang Gong Liquor now.

After generations' inheritance and development, the brewing techniques of Wenwang Gong Liquor became more and more mature. Especially after the founding of new China, the government rebuilt a local state-owned Linquan winery on the basis of "old workshop" to carry forward this ancient liquor brewing method made by five cereals. The new winery uses the old cellars and all the operations still follow the old brewing techniques, that are, layering the cereals, adding the cereals, steaming the liquor and sealing the cellar by mud all manually. In 1988, the brewer of Wenwang Gong Liquor combined the latest brewing technology with the traditional "five cereals" brewing techniques to form the exclusive separate steaming method, that is unique operation method of Wenwang Gong Liquor. This new method pushed the production techniques of Wenwang Gong Liquor to a new level, and the series fragrant liquor of Wenwang has been deeply loved by consumers.

In May 2014, Wenwang Gong Liquor Brewing entered the fourth list of province-level intangible cultural heritage representative items.

---

① "Su Shi" was a Chinese poet, writer, politician, calligrapher, painter, pharmacologist, and gastronome of the Song Dynasty (960–1279).

Zuisan Qiu Liquor Traditional Brewing (province-level)

The brewing techniques of Zuishan Qiu Liquor began in the Wei and Jin Dynasties (220-420). In the Song (960-1279) and Yuan (1271-1368) Dynasties, its fermentation and distiller's yeast techniques began to combine with distillation techniques. From the Ming (1368-1644) and Qing (1636-1912) Dynasties to the Republic of China (1912-1949), the brewing techniques were gradually improved and became mature. After the founding of the People's Republic of China, these brewing techniques have been protected and carried forward, forming unique processes of "one controlling process, three steaming processes and one preparing process" (controlling pulp to reduce water, steaming auxiliary material, steaming raw material, steaming liquor, and preparing cereals for fermentation) with the distinctive characteristics of "four highs and one medium" (high water temperature for moistening materials, high starch accumulation, high accumulation temperature, high water content in the fermentation room, and medium temperature to put cereals into the pottery jar).

Fig 24 The Brewing Processes of Zuisan Qiu Liquor

The name of Zuishan Qiu Liquor contains rich historical accumulation. It was said that Liu Ling, one of the "seven worthies of bamboo grove" in the Wei and Jin Dynasties (220-420), accompanied his literary friends to Yingzhou city (today's Fuyang) and walked into an alley with the fragrance of liquor. In the alley, it happened that Du Kang[①]'s descendants were making liquor and presented the liquor for them to taste. Liu Ling drank several bowls, got drunk and didn't wake up for three days. When he woke up on the fourth day, he exclaimed that "Had it been three years? and where am I now?". Du Kang's descendants were overjoyed and named this liquor as Yingzhou "Zuishan Qiu" (means got drunk for three autumns) since it was invented by Du Kang, the founder of liquor, without naming this liquor before. Therefore, today's Zuishan Qiu comes from the allusion of "Liu Ling got drunk after tasting liquor made by Du Kang". Ouyang Xiu[②], a famous writer of Song Dynasty whose art name Zuiweng (Chinese: 醉翁), had two hobbies when he was the governor of Yingzhou. One was to drink Zuishan Qiu Liquor that made Liu Ling drunk, and the other was to travel around West Lake of Yingzhou. Ouyang Xiu's poems contained the praise for liquor. These poems are world-renowned. Therefore, the Zuishan Qiu liquor produced by Anhui Golden Seed Winery Co., Ltd has a profound cultural history.

Anhui Golden Seed Winery Co., Ltd, formerly known as Fuyang Winery which was established in 1949, is a time-honored enterprise that inherits "Dasheng Liquor Shop" of Shanxi Merchants in Ming Dynasty (1368-1644) and "Yuntai Liquor Shop" of Shanxi Merchants in Republic of China (1912-1949). Up to now, the branches have preserved the ancient liquor-making cellars in the Ming (1368-1644) and Qing (1636-1912)

---

① "Du Kang" is one of the figures credited with the invention of alcoholic beverages in Chinese legend.

② "Ouyang Xiu" was a Chinese essayist, historian, poet, calligrapher, politician, and epigrapher of the Song Dynasty (960−1279).

Dynasties. These cellars are located on the bank of Ying River, the largest tributary of Huai River. With unique hydrological and geological conditions, this place is the birthplace of Hui Liquor ("Hui" is the abbreviation of Anhui province) and Yu Liquor ("Yu" is the abbreviation of Henan province) in the Central Plains and has been designated as "Cultural Relics Protection Unit" by the Anhui provincial government.

In 1987, Fuyang Zuishan Qiu Liquor was awarded premium product by the Ministry of Light Industry. The trademark of "Zuishan Qiu" was recognized as "Chinese Famous Trademark" by the Trademark Office of the State Administration for Industry and Commerce. At present, the series of liquor brand produced by Golden Seed Winery Co., Ltd, including "Golden Seeds", "Seed Liquor", "Yingzhou Liquor" and "Hetai Liquor", are all made by the traditional brewing of Zuishan Qiu. These liquors are also the national geographical indications protection products. The traditional brewing techniques of Zuishan Qiu Liquor has become a precious intangible cultural heritage of the liquor industry, with high scientific research value, economic development value and historical and cultural value.

In May 2014, Zuisan Qiu Liquor Traditional Brewing entered the fourth list of province-level intangible cultural heritage representative items.

Jinyu Wan Liquor Brewing (province-level)

Jinyu Wan Liquor is one of the most representative specialties in Jieshou city. Its brewing techniques originated from the North Song Dynasty (960-1127), and gradually improved and matured from the Ming (1368-1644) and Qing (1636-1912) Dynasties to the Republic of China (1912-1949).

After the founding of the People's Republic of China, the brewing techniques of Jinyu Wan Liquor has been protected and developed, forming unique processes of "three steaming processes, two controlling processes and one continuing process" (steaming auxiliary material, steaming raw material, steaming unfiltered liquor, controlling pulp to reduce acid, controlling pulp to reduce water, and continuing adding cereals for fermentation) with the distinctive characteristics of "four highs and one low" (high starch accumulation, high accumulation temperature, high water content in the fermentation room, high temperature for moistening materials and low temperature to put cereals into the pottery jar).

Fig 25 The Brewing Processes of Jinyu Wan Liquor

In recent years, Jinyu Wan Liquor has titled as "Anhui Green Food", "Anhui Time-honored Brand", "Anhui Top Ten Famous Liquor Brands", "Anhui Famous Brand Products", "Anhui Famous Trademark" and "Anhui Province New Products".

In November 2017, Jinyu Wan Liquor Brewing entered the fifth list of province-level intangible cultural heritage representative items.

Yingzhou Pillow Steamed Bun (province-level)

Pillow Steamed Bun, also known as Fuyang Steamed Bun, is about 10 to 15cm long, 5 to 8cm wide, and weighs about 2 to 6kg. It looks like a pillow and is one of the famous local specialties of Fuyang city. People call it as "the largest steamed bun in the world" and "the king of steamed bun worldwide".

The history of Pillow Steamed Bun of Yingzhou is long. It was said that during the great victory in Shunchang (now Fuyang city) of Song Dynasty (1140), in order to support the Song army to against Jin army, the local people steamed large buns in the shape of pillow and sent them to the barracks of Song army. Each soldier had one steamed bun. When they were hungry, they cut a piece of it to assuage their hunger. When they were sleepy, they could use this steamed bun as pillows to sleep. The name of "pillow steamed bun" comes from this. According to Hong Liangjun, the heritor of "Yingzhou Pillow Steamed Bun", his ancestors worked as an official to produce "Pillow Steamed Buns" for the army of Liu Qi, a famous anti-Jin army general. After generations of inheritance and improvement of the techniques, Pillow Steamed Bun has become today's Fuyang specialty.

Yingzhou district, located in the center of Fuyang city, is rich in high-quality wheat because of fertile land. This provides superior raw materials for the production of "Pillow Steamed Bun". Pillow Steamed Bun is fermented with rice wine and adopts local fine flour as principal material. The whole processes are divided into seven strict and exquisite steps of fermentation, flour mixing, flour rolling, weighing, kneading dough, resting dough, and steaming. The steamed buns are famous for their large size, mellow flavor, good taste and long-time storage.

Fig 26 Hong Chunliang is Making Yingzhou Pillow Steamed Buns

In Fuyang city alone, there are dozens of families specializing in steaming and selling this kind bun. Some of them even have set up companies whose business are prosperous. Among them, especially "Honghuzi Pillow Steamed Bun" is the first local company to obtain the trademark of Pillow Steamed Bun. Honghuzi Pillow Steamed Bun has the following characteristics. The first is that the bottom of steamed bun is golden yellow, which looks like fried. The second is that the whole bun is about half an inch thick with crisp and refreshing taste. If you cut a slice of it, you can see the bun is white and packed layer by layer. The third is that the bun is not dry and is easy to chew because of its softness and good texture. With no alkali, fermented powder and other substances before steaming, it will taste like fresh one without mold and desiccation after several days of storage. Pillow Steamed Bun had participated in national, provincial and municipal Food Fairs for many times, and won many honors. The relevant media and food programs at the state-level and province-level also reported it for many times.

At present, the production techniques of Yingzhou Pillow Steamed Bun have been widely spread with Fuyang city (Yingzhou) as the center, radiating to the surrounding areas of Bozhou city, Lu' an city, Taihe county, Jieshou county, Lixin county, Mengcheng county, and some areas in Henan province such as Zhoukou city and Huaibin county. Yingzhou Pillow Steamed Bun has become a daily household food for banquets and a good gift for visiting friends and relatives, which is widely welcomed.

In November 2017, Yingzhou Pillow Steamed Bun entered the fifth list of province-level intangible cultural heritage representative items.

Seven Quyi

Taihe Qinyin (province-level)

Taihe Qingyin has a long history. According to the records of *Music Score of Qingyin*, there was a monk whose religious name is Xuantan living on the south bank of Quan River in Yingzhou district at the beginning of Yuan Dynasty and the end of Ming Dynasty (1364-1368). He was knowledgeable and proficient in music. He liked to sing while playing instruments, especially the Chinese zither. He practiced all day long with perseverance. Later, he took a kind of melody as a song, playing and singing with the disciples every day. Because of its elegant melody, it is called Qingyin.

Taihe county has a profound history and culture. It is the hometown of calligraphy, painting, poem and poetry. The ground and development of Qingyin profits from this situation. In the early stage, Qingyin was only sung in temples. Later, it was spread by literati and refined scholars and came out of the "temple gate" and gradually became popular among scholars and wealthy families. In the middle of Qing Dynasty (1436-1566), Qingyin spread to Taihe county and was welcomed by ordinary people, so the spontaneous "Qingyin club" came into being. This club regulated that it was usually ten days or half a month for the concert, and the concert will perform in the wedding, birthday, opening and other joyous occasions. The concert was often held in the living room or courtyard. The performers sit around the table, each holding an instrument for a role, singing while playing with enjoyment.

Qingyin club, this form soon became popular on both sides of Ying

River after it was performed in Taihe county, and spread to Fuyang city, Bozhou city, Lixin county, Guoyang county, Mengcheng county and some areas in Henan province, such as Shenqiu county, Xincai county, Luyi county, Taikang county. In some festive dates, such as succeeding in a government examination, the completion of a new house, the opening of the business, the elder's birthday, the birth of a baby, these masters will invite Qingyin club to perform for congratulations, which became a major local custom.

Fig 27 Some Old artists Are Performing Taihe Qinyin with Some Instruments

Taihe Qingyin is elegant, beautiful and melodious, which belongs to an elegant music. Originated in Taihe county of Fuyang which located in the Northern Anhui, it belongs to the quyi of Central Plains. But its singing style is quite different from some operas in the Northern China. The operas in the Northern China are always high-pitched, bold and rough, while Taihe Qingyin is graceful and elegant with unique artistic characteristics which are the reasons why it has been popular all the time.

After the founding of the People's Republic of China, Taihe Qingyin got more attention, and some veteran artists reperformed again. In 1954, the Cultural Center of Taihe county organized veteran Qingyin artists to set up an amateur troupe, which took the lead in changing Qingyin playing and singing into opera performance. In 1958, the traditional repertoire of Taihe Qingyin, *Chasing Boat* participated in the First Provincial Quyi Performance and won the prize. In August of the same year, the only "Qingyin Opera Troupe" nationwide was established in Taihe county. After sorting out and innovating, the troupe arranged some programs which were toured all over the province and were widely popular. The troupe has participated in provincial and municipal art performances for many times and won many awards. Anhui Broadcasting Corporation had recorded Qingyin and broadcasted it in selected venues and time periods.

In the early 1960s, this opera troupe was once abolished, and Qingyin artists and performances gradually disappeared. After the reform and opening up, Taihe Qingyin has been revitalized. The local government actively supported the restoration of amateur organization and activities of Qingyin, attached importance to the protection of heritors and the cultivation of new talents, and built performance stages. In 2013, Taihe Qingyin entered the classroom for the first time, took root in many secondary vocational schools. Meanwhile, such artists as Zhang Hongkui, the provincial heritor of Taihe Qingyin, and Yu Fei, the municipal heritor, emerged too.

In December 2006, Taihe Qingyin entered the first list of province-level intangible cultural heritage representative items.

Jieshou Yugu (province-level)

Jieshou Yugu (a percussion instrument made of bamboo), also called as Daotongzi or Zhuiziweng in Chinese, has a jargon which was called "liulan tiaoer" in Chinese. It is the predecessor of Daoqing Opera which is a rare local opera in China and serves as one of the original operas of Zhuizi Opera in Henan province. Originated in the Ming Dynasty (1368-1644) and flourished in the Qing Dynasty (1636-1912), Yugu has a history of more than 400 years. It is known as the "living fossil" of operas in the Sha River and Ying River basin, which has important reference value for the study of local operas and related operas.

Its source should come from the "narrative-singing Daoqing Opera" of Ming Dynasty (1368-1644). This narrative-singing opera belongs to the tunes of admonishing and educating the masses and self-cultivation sung by wandering Taoists and Taoist nuns. After spreading to Jieshou city, this opera combined with local folk tunes. After generations of inheritance, innovation and development by artists, Jieshou Yugu formed. It mainly spread in Fuyang area, and some areas in Henan province such as Zhoukou city and Shangqiu city.

During the Daoguang reign (1821-1850) in Qing Dynasty, Jieshou Yugu flourished. At that time, the outstanding artists included Wang Deqing, Guo Wo and Chang Yuande, etc. In the thirty-first year of Guangxu reign (1905) in Qing Dynasty, there were female artists who set up stalls for singing Yugu. Among them, Gu Xihua and Fu Guixi were the most famous. During this period, the artists intended to combine Jieshou Yugu with the local popular opera called as "Yingheliu", forming a new singing method which was welcomed by the audience. After this singing method was spread to Henan province, the famous folk quyi, "Henan

Zhuizi Opera" was formed.

In the 1930s and 1940s, Jieshou Yugu was in its heyday. Many artists appeared at that time with more than ten famous artists which include Xu Fengshan, Liang Fengxing, Xu Guangzhen and Xu Zhibang. Plays such as *Sister Yu's Congratulations on Birthday* and *Beat Lian Ke* were all the rage. During the Anti-Japanese War, Jieshou was once known as "a little Shanghai" in the rear battlefield because of its special geographical location with transport wharf. The busy business and increasing demand for entertainment also provided conditions for the development of Jieshou Yugu. At that time, more than 20 Yugu troupes performed at the same time, which contributed this art as one of "three major operas" with Henan Zhuizi Opera and Huaibei Bangzi Opera.

Fig 28 Musical Instrument: Yugu

Originated and developed from the folk, Jieshou Yugu has distinctive characteristics because it integrated with a variety of local arts, such as Zhuizi Opera and Grum Storytelling. For the terrain of Jieshou city is long and narrow from north to south, there are two kinds of Yugu. In the south, it is called "high-pitched Yugu" and in the north, it is called "low-pitched Yugu". Their common features are that the performance is mainly based on singing, supplemented by narrative-singing, rhymes are added in lyrics and spoken parts with mellow, natural and beautiful singing. Most of the themes are classical traditional operas which include short "shumao" (refers to the short part of songs before the singing) for having fun and long "dashu" (refers to the main singing part) for praising justice and denouncing ugliness. These themes reflect the simplicity of folk customs, the goodness and beauty of human nature, and the profoundness of culture. This art is also well-received. Artists are mostly male, so their singing is either loud and clear, or euphemistic and low. They are good at creating vivid, emotional and moving atmosphere. They often stop abruptly when the key plot is reached, so that the audience is attracted by the plot and will come uninvited.

When performing, one person finishes all the opera, which is not limited by time and space. The instruments are very simple. The performer holds a Yugu, commonly called as Daotongzi in Chinese, which is a processed bamboo, about 120cm long and 6cm in diameter. The other instrument is a simple board, which is composed of two strip boards. When singing, the artist beat the Yugu with one hand and played the simple board with the other hand, which is easy to operate and use.

After the founding of People's Republic of China, Jieshou Yugu got a certain degree of inheritance. The restoration of the local "Miaohu Folk Art Fair" has also set up a new platform for the performance of Jieshou Yugu and has promoted the development of this art. In 1958, Xu Zhibang, an artist of Yugu, took part in the First Quyi Performance in Anhui province. His play *A Pair of Red Flowers* won the second prize in the singing group. Since the new era, due to the influence and impact of various media, the performance market of Jieshou Yugu has shrunk seriously. In order to rescue this endangered folk art, the government has carried out activities such as inviting heritors to come to the campus for Yugu training. In 1995, the repertoire performed by Miao Qingchen, the heritor of Jieshou Yugu, won the prize in the Third Provincial Art Festival and entered the CCTV opera channel.

In December 2006, Jieshou Yugu entered the first list of province-level intangible cultural heritage representative items.

Huai River Qinshu (province-level)

Qinshu, commonly called as "Yangqin" in Chinese, got its name because its main accompaniment instrument is "Yangqin". The main popular spread areas are Funan county of Fuyang, Si county of Suzhou city, Lu'an city, Chuzhou city, Bengbu city and Bozhou city. In the 1930s, it was called "Anhui Qinshu".

According to archaeological research, Huai River Qinshu was first introduced into Funan county by ecdemic performers, with a history of more than 200 years. There are three ways of introduction. Firstly, it was introduced from Dang Mountain (a mountain located in Suzhou city in the northernmost part of Anhui province), and the representative heritors included Shao Yuanzhen, a veteran artist in Yongcheng county of Henan province, and Meng Zhaoxing, Meng Xianchun, Meng Ying, etc.; Secondly, it was introduced from a blind person of Shandong province (whose real name is unknown), and the representative heritors included Yang Yuande, Zhang Fa, Miao Mingcai, Yuan Jinbang, etc.; Thirdly, it was taught by local masters of Qinshu, and the representative heritors included some people without knowing their real names, such as Chen Huoya ("huoya" is the stage name, which means there are gaps between one's teeth), Liang Mazi ("mazi" is the stage name, which means one's face has many pocks), some people with real names, such as Fu Xuelan, Wang Wenyi. In order to meet the cultural needs of the local people, all kinds of Qinshu artists learned from each other and integrated Huaici Opera, bass drum, Zhuizi Opera and other folk tunes, gradually forming a unique art of quyi called as Huai River Qinshu. This art can represent the customs of Hua River, and began to spread in the Huai River Basin and Northern Anhui area.

Fig 29 Musical Instrument: Qinshu

Although the introduction sources of Huai River Qinshu are different. But in a word, it is mainly composed of tunes. The representative tunes are "four-sentence tune" and "Duoziban① tune". The former can be divided into "slow four-sentence tune" and "fast four-sentence tune "; In the middle of the "Duoziban tune", there is a narrative-speaking after singing. Besides, there are also other tunes such as "Fengyangge" and "Meihualuo". People called the singing of Huai River Qinshu as "nine tunes and eighteen accents". Huaihe Qinshu has unique artistic features. Its melody is graceful, singing is slow and thick, words is simple and vivid, which are full of beautiful and long-lasting charm with strong local flavor. Among the numerous folk operas in the Huai River basin, it is unique and deeply loved by the masses. Representative plays include *Wang Tianbao Goes to Suzhou, Chen Sanliang Climbs in the Court, Borrows Umbrella When Strolling Lake* and so on.

The performance of Huai River Qinshu is relatively simple. The performer plays the board with one hand and the other hand with Qinshu,

---

① "Duoziban" is a kind of plate-type of opera singing.

accompanied by a band. There are two or more people singing, and other actors performing on the stage. The forms of performance are flexible and diverse, which are loved by the masses. In the early years, there were hundreds of people sitting on the ground to watch the performances, which was very spectacular. There were also indoor performances in teahouses and other places, where the audience enjoyed tea while watching opera, which became a kind of elegant enjoyment. Huaihe Qinshu was very popular in towns of Funan county during the Ming (1368-1644) and Qing (1636-1912) Dynasties.

After the founding of the People's Republic of China, Huai River Qinshu has developed healthily and orderly. The government advocated the creation new plays. A number of outstanding performing talents have emerged, such as Yuan Yue'e, Lu Caixia and Zhang Jing. They have won relevant awards issued by provincial and municipal cultural departments for many times. During the "Great Cultural Revolution" (1966-1976), the Huai River Qinshu was impacted and withered for a time. Since the reform and opening up, Huai River Qinshu has been revitalized and reactive in various stages of Huai River Basin. It has participated in the rehearsal and performance organized by superior authorities and won many awards. At the same time, many outstanding actors have emerged, such as Meng Ying, the provincial representative heritor and the winner of "Peony Award" which is the highest award of Chinese Quyi.

In November 2008, Huai River Qinshu entered the second list of province-level intangible cultural heritage representative items.

Shoulder Pole Show (province-level)

Shoulder Pole Show, commonly called as "xiaodiaozi" in Chinese, is also called as monkey-body with person's head, solo show and one-legged show. At the end of the Qing Dynasty, Ge San, an artist of Lixin county, introduced this into villages of Jieshou city and blended with local folk art to form a new performance form with a history of more than 100 years.

It was said that Shoulder Pole Show originated in Xiaoxu village of Jieshou city. In order to make a living, the local people had the tradition of going out to do monkey show and singing in exchange for food and clothing. During the Tongzhi reign (1862-1875) of the Qing Dynasty, Ge San, an artist of Lixin county, went to Jieshou to perform the Shoulder Pole Show from door to door. When he went to the Xiaoxu village, he got cold and was taken care of by a villager called Zhu Huixian. In return, Ge San taught this art to the Zhu's family after recovery.

Zhu Huixian mastered what Ge San had taught and quickly grasped the traditional performing skills of the Shoulder Pole Show. He didn't keep his back on himself, but boldly innovated the traditional "Shoulder Pole Show" and absorbed the essence of the local quyi, forming the unique style of Shoulder Pole Show of Jieshou. He also became the first-generation heritor of "Jieshou Shoulder Pole Show".

After the founding of the People's Republic of China, Zhu Xuelun and Zhu Yunde, two artists of Xiaoxu village carried forward the Shoulder Pole Show and innovated its performing skills. The father and son learned from other people's advantages, made puppets and props, created figures painted on clothes by clay, and created programs. With historical stories, myths and legends, fables and traditional operas as the themes, the new plays aimed at upholding justice, punishing the evil, promoting the good figures for helping others. The two artists also integrated the light and flexible performance form of traditional shoulder pole show into the plays, so that the common people can enjoy it and be inspired by education after watching the performance. Their plays include traditional plays, such as *Wang Xiaoer Selling Tofu*, *Wang Xiaoer Beating Tiger*, *Xianglian Suing*, *Ma Hulun Exchanging Marriage*, and modern plays, such as *Catching Secret Agents*, *Divorce of Young Couple*. The performances were welcomed by the local audience and spread to more than ten counties and cities at the junction area of Henan province, Anhui province and Jiangsu province, which led to the development and growth of Shoulder Pole Show of Xiaoxu village even the whole area of Jieshou city. Influenced by it, many people started to learn and spread this art, and Jieshou Shoulder Pole Show reached its peak.

Fig 30 Some Figures Made by Shoulder Poles

In 1980, Zhu Yunde, a veteran artist of Jieshou Shoulder Pole Show joined the quyi troupe and became the leader. He led the troupe to "make a performance tour" in Anhui province, Shandong province, Henan province and other places. When they performed in a place where the audience was full. Many media from Anhui province and other provinces interviewed and reported on the troupe. Zhu Yunde's troupe has also participated in the First Provincial Folk Culture and Art Festival, the city's "Double-Arts Festival" and other performances for more than 100 times, which were well received by the society.

In recent years, due to the influence of market economy and entertainment environment, the number of practitioners of Jieshou Shoulder Pole Show has decreased because of the shrunk market. Only a few veteran artists are still sticking to this art. There is a long way to go for the rescue and inheritance of this traditional folk art.

In December 2008, Jieshou Shoulder Pole Show entered the second list of province-level intangible cultural heritage representative items.

Yingshang Bass Drum Storytelling (province-level)

Yingshang Bass Drum Storytelling, commonly known as "playing drum while telling stories", is a traditional folk art which is performed by solo speaking and singing. It has a long history for more than two hundred years, which can be traced back to the mid-Qing Dynasty (1728-1820). This art is a distinctive folk art form in Ying-Huai area.

Yingshang Bass Drum Storytelling is popular in Funan county and Huoqiu county of Huai River basin. According to *Anhui Volume of Chinese Quyi Annals*, "Li Jiasheng, the heritor of Yingshang Bass Drum Storytelling, learned this art from artist Zhu Huating when he was 18 years old. He devoted himself to studying this art and realized solo performance when he was 20 years old. He lived in Yingshang for a long time after performed a lot in Fuyang city, Huoqiu county, Yingshang county and Funan county. The paper, *Research on the Historical Development of Drum Storytelling of Anhui Province* also describes the birth and inheritance of Yingshang Bass Drum Storytelling. It says that "Bass Drum Storytelling was promoted and spread in the area where Li Jiasheng lived in with Yingshang county as the center.

Fig 31 Bass Drum and An Old Artist is Performing

The art form of Bass Drum Storytelling combines singing and stories telling, which belongs to a kind of improvisation, that is, making up stories according to the scene. With its high-pitched, tactful singing and humorous words, it has always been popular. In order to attract the audience, artists also broadened the theme and began to "tell a series of stories", that was, singing and speaking literary masterpieces, historical stories. Given this, Bass Drum Storytelling is rich in local culture, ethnical characteristics and folk literature value. Singing is rough with rigorous lyrics, plain tone, elegant harmony and standard structure. Especially the suspense left by the artist, makes plots exciting. In most cases, a long story will have many suspense which can be divided into great suspense and general ones. The great suspense will pave the way for the coming general one and vice versa, which makes the audience attracted by the plot of the story.

Bass drum, drum rack and castanets are all the performers' instruments of Yingshang Bass Drum Storytelling, which are easy to play. Whether the themes come from the popular folk novels related to historical romance, martial arts and complicated legal cases, or from the literature related to Anti-Japanese War, War of Liberation and heroes of wars after the founding of new China, they can be spread by drum storytelling, which plays a positive role in publicizing social justice and promoting positive energy. In the 1980s and 1990s, artists of Yingshang Bass Drum Storytelling performed in the villages where the transportation was poor and the information was closed along the Huai River. They set up performance to provide spiritual nourishment for the farmers in these remote areas.

In May 2014, Yingshang Bass Drum Storytelling entered the fourth list of province-level intangible cultural heritage representative items.

Yingshang Qinshu (province-level)

Yingshang Qinshu has a history of more than 300 years. In the early years, it widely aborded the essence of Shandong Qinshu, Xuzhou Qinshu, Qinshu in Eastern Henan province and Huai River Qinshu. Eventually, it became an independent folk art singing form in the late Qing Dynasty and the early Republic of China (1900-1920).

Yingshang Qinshu pays attention to the combination with local folk songs, tunes and flower-drum lantern dance, and integrates the operas of surrounding areas. After Li Jiasheng, a veteran artist of Yingshang county, standardized art pedigree, and integrated the mature techniques of holding hardwood clapper and twisting drumstick in Yingshang Bass Drum Storytelling into Yingshang Qinshu. Finally, the unique performance style of Yingshang Qinshu was established. This also formed different characteristics of Yingshang Bass Drum Storytelling and Yingshang Qinshu within one the same school. Yingshang Qinshu has been handed down for four generations.

Fig 32 A Female Artist is Performing Yingshang Qinshu

The plate-type structure of Yingshang Qinshu is mainly from the tunes of Huai River Qinshu, and its representative tune is "four-sentence tune". The "four-sentence tune" can be divided into "slow four-sentence tune" and "fast four-sentence tune"; In the middle of the "Duoziban tune", there is a narrative-speaking after singing. Besides, there are also some tunes such as "Fengyangge" and "Meihualuo". Artists called this as "Nine tunes and eighteen accents". In terms of singing, Yingshang Qinshu has strong local characteristics, accompanied by Chinese dulcimer, urheen (urhheen), hardwood clapper and so on. There are three kinds of performance forms which include solo, alternately singing and group singing. Solo means one person needs to finish the performance with urheen on the hand, accompanied by hardwood clapper under the foot. Alternately singing means a man and a woman sings alternatively, with man playing the urheen and woman playing the Chinese dulcimer or hardwood clapper. Group singing means more than three people sing together, with one playing the Chinese dulcimer or hardwood clapper, the others playing the urheen and singing in different roles.

Yingshang Qinshu has a wide influence in the area along the Huai River because of its graceful melody, slow and thick singing, simple and vivid language, lively singing form, rich regional characteristics and artistic appeal. In the new era, with the development of economy and society, Yingshang Qinshu has been impacted by the diversification of local entertainment and market economy, and has become a local cultural heritage on the verge of extinction. The local cultural department has launched rescue work.

In November 2017, Yingshang Qinshu entered the fifth list of province-level intangible cultural heritage representative items.

Eight Folklore

Miaohu Folk Art Fair (state-level)

Originated in the Jiaqing reign (1796-1821) of the Qing Dynasty, Jieshou Folk Art Fair has a history of more than 200 years with originally name as "Miaohu Narrative-singing Fair". It was initiated by Miao Benlin, the farmer and artist of Zhuizi Opera in Miaohu village of Renzhai town, Jieshou city.

In the past, Miaohu village used to be a poor village with low-lying terrain. It was flooded twice in three years, rare to have a harvest. At the beginning of June of the lunar calendar, farmers who had harvested wheat and planted beans, will put aside their hoes to seek spiritual nourishments after meal. In order to celebrate the harvest, pray for good fortune, and express their feelings, the versatile Miao Benlin took the lead and sat on the stage to sing songs and tell stories with instruments. At the beginning, only several artists from the village participated in this art fair. Gradually, artists from neighboring villages came to perform, and the programs became more and more abundant, attracting more and more audience.

What was valuable was that in the following hundred years, whether it was the peaceful years of a golden harvest or the hard days of war, "Miaohu Folk Art Fair" was passed down from generation to generation without interruption. Miao Hezhu, the second-generation heritor, Miao Jiaode, the third-generation heritor, and Miao Yongfen, the fourth-generation heritor, had carried forward this art fair in their hometown in succession. In 1939, Miao Yuanfu, the sixth-generation heritor, held a large-scale art fair to commemorate the 165th anniversary of the birth of

Miao Benlin, the founder. He invited many artists to participate in the performance and welcomed the people of neighboring villages to watch. He and his colleagues agreed that "Miaohu Folk Art Fair" will hold regularly in the sixth day of the sixth lunar month in a leap year, which lasts for five days.

Since then, through continuous inheritance, Miaohu Folk Art Fair had made great progresses. Miaohu village, an ordinary small village, has become a gathering place for artists and a stage for mass entertainment under the great efforts of many generations of artists of Miao family. During the "Great Cultural Revolution" (1966-1976), influenced by the "left-leaning" trend of thought, the art fair was once withered. The reform and opening up has brought opportunities for the Miaohu Folk Art Fair to be full of vitality. The famous artist, Miao Qingchen, the seventh-generation heritor, saw that people's material life has improved, but their cultural life was very poor. Inspired by the "Majie Folk Art Fair", he made strong efforts to recover the art fair. He ran around to contact artists, and held a three-day art fair that year. More than 30 famous artists from 9 counties and cities in Henan province and Anhui province participated, which had a great influence. After seeing the new hope, the next year, Miao Qingchen continued to contact famous artists in surrounding counties and cities to restart the Miaohu Folk Art Fair which was not held before for a long time. After the information was released, quyi artists from Fuyang city, Cao county in Shandong province, Shao county in Jiangsu province, Dawu county in Hubei province and Zhoukou city in Henan province attended the fair one after another, holding a great art fair never seen before. Ma Yuping, a famous artist of Henan Zhuizi Opera, and many famous artists went to Miaohu Folk Art Fair to perform. In terms of programs, this fair enlarged from Zhuizi Opera only in the beginning to nearly 50 kinds of arts at present which include Yu Opera, Bian Lian[①], Xihe Bass Drum Storytelling, Yingshang Flower-drum Lantern Dance, Northern Anhui Bass Drum Storytelling, Qinshu, Storytelling, Song-and-dance Duet, Crosstalk, Allegro, Haizi Opera, Yugu and so on. In addition, there are also some folk dances such as Lion Dancing and Dry-boat Dancing with rich content.

Fig 33 Annual Miaohu Folk Art Fair in 2008

"Speaking at all the time, singing around all the places, and all the people enjoy" is not only the self-entertainment feature of Miaohu folk art fair, but also the true portrayal of its original interest. The programs are performed in Miaohu folk art fair, especially Zhuizi Opera and Stroytelling, with simple props and easy to sing, which is not limited by the place and time. The sincere and simple singing is especially suitable for farmers' cultural needs. In addition to the traditional plays include *The*

① "Bian Lian" is an ancient Chinese dramatic art. Performers wear vividly colored masks, typically depicting well known characters from the opera, which they change from one face to another almost instantaneously with the swipe of a fan, a movement of the head, or wave of the hand.

Story of Golden Whip, *The Biography of Bandits*, *The Big Red Robe* and *The Bama Mountain*. There are also 106 new plays and more than 150 new plays newly created in the new era. The works created by Miao Qingchen and Zhang Hongyou have won many awards.

With its profound culture and sincere, simple art form, Miaohu Folk Art Fair is deeply loved by the masses. It also builds a platform for spiritual and material exchanges. This fair makes positive contributions to eulogize the Party's policies of poverty alleviation, build the new trend of rural civilization, and publicize the socialist core values and cultural revitalization. At the same time, the exchange of agricultural and sideline products is active during the art fair. The village becomes a prosperous market at the fair, which effectively promoted the local economic development. *People's Daily*, *People's Daily Overseas Edition*, CCTV and other media have published and reported the grand occasion of Miaohu Folk Art Fair.

In June 2008, Miaohu Folk Art Fair entered the second list of state-level intangible cultural heritage representative items.

Linquan Taige and Zhouge (state-level)

As a kind of comprehensive art form that uses dance as the main part and integrates music, opera, acrobatics and painting, Yingshang Taige and Zhouge is a kind of unique folk dance which comes from folk life and close to people's life, with strong local characteristics and vitality. In the Northwestern Anhui province, it has a broad mass base and has the reputation of "air dance".

Fig 34 The Performing Pictures of Taige and Zhouge

Linquan county has the honorary title of "the Hometown of Chinese Folk Culture and Art", with profound cultural accumulation. The performance of Taige and Zhouge has a long history. The earliest performance of Taige and Zhouge appeared in the middle Ming Dynasty (1436-1566). At that time, it was a kind of self-entertainment art form created by local people during their labor time. The characteristic is that people perform dance on a kind of small flow "stage" created by themselves. The unique performance and simple operation of this art make it very suitable for the people who live in plains to watch. According to Zhang Defang, the late senior citizen of Zhangguan town of Lingquan county, who heard from his predecessors that in the middle Ming Dynasty there were a group of people who performed Taige and Zhouge in the bazaars of Yangqiao town, Zhangguan town and other towns. Their performance was so popular so that all the people went out to watch this art.

Zhouge derived from Tuoge. The appearance of Tuoge was to fix the problem of stage. Because the local area was located in a plain, the people who were outside the performance could't see the performance clearly. Therefore, the artists carried the younger ones on their back to perform, which is called Tuoge. Tuoge further developed into Zhouge. The performance of Zhouge can be divided into two parts. The upper part is the performer, most of them are young children with light weight. The lower part is the supporter, which is composed of strong young men with iron shelf on their body to form a unique "stage" that can walk around. The children can dance and play on the "stage". In order to lighten the burden of the supporter and expand the performance lineup, artists tried to change the iron shelf into a square table, with 4-8 people carrying the square table. A square table is an independent stage which can move around and accommodate many performers.

In the beginning, the performance of Taige and Zhouge was simple in operation. The purpose was purely to pray for fortune and avoid disaster. The performance was mostly performed at temple fairs. As time goes on, folk artists made improvement through integrating operas, acrobatics, song and dance performances into this art. Taige has gradually become a kind of cultural and entertainment program, which can be performed on various occasions, especially in traditional festivals such as Spring Festival, Lantern Festival, Dragon Boat Festival, Mid-Autumn Festival and other celebrations. Taige and Zhouge looks like a twin that is inseparable from each other. During the performance, Taige is often performed in front of Zhouge. With the cooperation of the "eight instrument class" (gong, cymbal, bass drum, side drum, sheng (mouth reed organ), xiao (vertical flute) and di (horizontal flute)), the performance is lively and spectacular with coherent plays Most of the audience can be affected by the performance atmosphere and deeply moved by the content.

The plays of Linquan Taige and Zhouge are rich. Traditional plays are mostly based on historical allusions, literary masterpieces, legends and stories. Then these stories are processed by artists, with the themes of praising the true, the good and the beautiful, and flogging the false and the ugly. These plays include *The Flood into Jinshan Temple*, *Celestial Beauty Scattering Flowers*, *The Fairy Comes Down to Earth*, *Come Back to Jingzhou* and *Wu Song Fights the Tiger*. The modern plays include *The Bay of Liu River*, *The Wreath Under the Mountain*, etc. There are also some plays for pure entertainment, such as *Liu Hai Playing with Golden Toads*, which are also well-received by the local people.

In June 2008, Linquan Taige and Zhouge entered the second list of state-level intangible cultural heritage representative items.

Jieshou Dahuang Temple Fair (province-level)

Temple fair is an ancient traditional folk custom and folk religious cultural activity. Jieshou Dahuang Temple Fair began in the Tang Dynasty (618-907) and flourished in the Ming Dynasty (1368-1644). It is held on March 26th of the lunar calendar every year for as long as 10 days. It has a long history and far-reaching influence.

Fig 35 Some Pictures of Dahuang Temple Fair

Fu Xi, courtesy name Taihao (Chinese: 太昊), is the ancestor of humanity in myth, and later generations call him as "the first ancestor". It was said that after unifying the tribes, Fu Xi established his regime in Huaiyang county of Henan province. Later, due to the flooding of the Yellow River, he moved the regime to Dahuang town of Jieshou city, Anhui province. Seeing that Dahuang town was located at a higher altitude with broad vision, fertile land and honest folk customs, Fu Xi set up a second capital to develop tribes here. When the flood receded and everything returned to normal, Fu Xi unfortunately dided at Dahuang town. Local people were very sad, so they used a good coffin to put his body and prepared an elaborate funeral. When they lifted the coffin, they couldn't lift it. Wizard told everyone that it was because Fu Xi was willing to leave his head here. As a result, his head was buried in Dahuang town, and his body was transported back to Huaiyang county.

In order to commemorate Fu Xi, later generations built up temples to sacrifice him. The two temples were built in Huaiyang of Henan and Jieshou of Anhui respectively, and the temple fairs were held in two places. The former was called Huaiyang Temple Fair, and the latter was called Dahuang Temple Fair. The former was held on the 2nd day of the second month of the lunar calendar, which is the date of the return of Fu Xi. The latter was held on the 26th day of the third month of the lunar calendar, which is the date of the burial of Fu Xi. The dates of two fairs are similar with the same origin and person to sacrifice.

The first day of the Dahuang Temple Fair was the opening ceremony for burning incense. People in Taoist costumes held colorful flags. Amid the noise of gongs and drums, they beat drum and bronze bell three times respectively. Then the chief worshipper chanted scriptures and prayed for God's blessing to the people. This ceremony had been continued. In the 13th year of Kaiyuan (725) of Tang Dynasty, the Dahuang Temple was rebuilt on the original site for the first time, and rebuilt again in Yuan Dynasty (1271-1368). The scale of the temple expanded continuously, covering an area of more than 100 mu (about 66666 square meters), with more than 100 halls and rooms. The facilities in the hall were magnificent with endless stream of pilgrims.

After the founding of the People's Republic of China, the Dahuang Temple was forcibly demolished in movement of breaking "Four Olds"①. During the "Great Cultural Revolution"(1966-1976), the statues of Fu Xi and other Gods were all destroyed. In 1998, in order to meet the needs of ancestor worship, the mausoleum of Fu Xi was rebuilt, and the Dahuang Temple was repaired and expanded through restoration of four halls and eastern and western corridors. The main part of the temple is divided into Fu Xi Hall and Fu Xi Mausoleum. The hall includes some towers, pavilions and temples, such as Shennong② Tower, Zhonggu③ Tower, Sanguan④ Pavilion, Ancestor Hall⑤, Guan Yu⑥ Hall, Wumu⑦ Temple. At the same time, the Dahuang Temple Fair restored the traditional sacrifice, and the activities were held in the hall.

Because Fu Xi was the "first ancestor" and taught people to sow and cultivate land and control population reproduction, the Dahuang Temple Fair has become a typical folk festival of ancestor worship, and the local area has gradually become the core space and holy land of Fu Xi Culture

---

① breaking "Four Olds" refer to get rid of old ideas, old culture, old customs and old habits.

② "Shennong", variously translated as "Divine Farmer" or "Divine Husbandman", was a mythological Chinese ruler who has become a deity in Chinese and Vietnamese folk religion. He is venerated as a culture hero in China and Vietnam.

③ "Zhonggu" refers to ancient ritual instruments.

④ In Chinese mythology, the Sanguan Dadi (三官大帝) are three emperor officials who judge humanity under the command of the Jade Emperor.

⑤ "Ancestor Hall" means the hall of Fu Xi.

⑥ "Guan Yu", courtesy name Yunchang, was a Chinese military general serving under the warlord Liu Bei during the late Eastern Han dynasty of China. Along with Zhang Fei, he shared a brotherly relationship with Liu Bei and accompanied him on most of his early exploits.

⑦ "Wumu" is used in posthumous titles of many emperors and generals.

in the Central Plains. People worship here and integrate songs, dances and music together to form fixed activities such as touching the hole of stone kiln, meeting at hall entrance, watching burning incense, burning fragrant eggs, tying descendants and begging mud dogs. In the atmosphere of temple fair culture, pilgrims are edified. They pray and dance for peace and a bumper harvest, get enlightenment, and wish the prosperity of motherland.

Nowadays, the content of Dahuang Temple Fair is more abundant, which is not only a cultural landscape, but also a folk cultural landscape. During the temple fair, in addition to the solemn and sacred traditional ancestor worship activities, other cultural entertainment such as operas and dances are also wonderful. The performances of dragon dancing, dry-boat dancing and acrobatic glut tourists' eyes. A wide range of clay dogs, cloth tigers, flower sticks, peach spears and other crafts make people eye opening. High-altitude acrobatics, magic stunts, artists' narrative-singing and instrumental performance are amazing. At the same time, commodity trade and material exchange are increasingly frequent. Its influence area extends to Anhui province, Henan province, Shandong province, Jiangsu province and other cities and provinces. According to statistics, more than 300000 people came to participate in the temple fair.

In December 2008, Jieshou Dahuang Temple Fair entered the second list of province-level intangible cultural heritage representative items.

Yingzhou Zhouge (province-level)

Yingzhou Zhouge is one of the traditional folk dances with unique local characteristics. According to the local veteran artists, it was formed in the middle of the Qing Dynasty (178-1820) and created by Wang Xing, a dance master from Yuanji town of Yingzhou district. He created this art on the basis of the old folk dance "Tuoge" after reform and innovation.

Originated from Yuanji town of Yingzhou district and Zhuzhai town of Funan county, Yingzhou Zhouge spreads to many counties in southern Fuyang, and extends to Fengtai county, Shou county, Bengbu, as well as some areas in Henan province. It is an ancient traditional folk dance that spreads across the two provinces along the Huai River and deeply loved by the masses.

Fig 36 Children are Performing above Taige

In terms of performance, Yingzhou Zhouge has many similarities and mutual adoption when it compares with Linquan Taige and Zhouge. At the same time, as a local art that has been preserved for hundreds of years, Yingzhou Zhouge not only retains many performance skills and original style of "Tuoge" which is almost lost, but also blazes a trail on high-altitude performance. It plays a transitional role in the evolution of the three traditional folk dances (Tuoge-Zhouge-Taige). Therefore, it also reflects the essence of local traditional culture more vividly and completely, and serves as one of the "living specimens" of Fuyang folk culture today.

The instruments of Yingzhou Zhouge are simple. The accompaniment band is generally composed of 5-6 people. The musical instruments include bass drum and side drum, bass gong and gong, big cymbal and small cymbal, etc. The artistic images are mostly based on the famous works such as *Journey to the West*, *Water Margin*, *The Romance of the Three Kingdoms* and some traditional opera plays. In recent years, it has added a number of plays full of modern life atmosphere and close to people's life, which are welcomed by the masses.

In December 2008, Yingzhou Zhouge entered the second list of province-level intangible cultural heritage representative items.

Zhang Clan Ancestral Hall Worship (province-level)

Zhang Clan Ancestral Hall is located at Zhanglaojia village which is about 5km away from the northern Tanpeng town of Linquan county, next to Jiulong town of Yingzhou district in the east, and next to Gaotang town of Linquan county in the south and west. The ancestral hall was built by Zhang Biao, the great-grandson of the Zhang family. He is a "Gongsheng" (ancient scholar recommended by local government) of the Ming Dynasty (1368-1644). This hall has lasted for more than 500 years.

Fig 37 The Ancestral Worship Activities of the Zhang Clan

The ancestral worship of the Zhang clan originated in the Ming Dynasty (1368-1644) and flourished in the Qing Dynasty (1636-1912) and the Republic of China (1912-1949). According to the ancestral genealogy, the ancestors of the Zhang clan migrated from Shandong province to Linquan county and settled in Zhanglaojia village, forming "four big families". Later, this clan has been thriving. Up to now, the whole Zhang clan has a population of nearly 100000, which is actually a famous clan in the local area.

The ancestral worship activities of the Zhang clan are held in the Zhang Clan Ancestral Hall on February 28th of the lunar calendar every year. In the early years, the ancestral worship activities were in turn held by the "four big families" once in every four years. According to the clan' s rules, no matter which family is in turn, it is necessary to kill "five animals" (cattle, sheep, pig, dog and chicken) to worship ancestors, and prepare goods and banquets serving for the worshippers. Prepared things need to be put in the kitchen in advance. During the worship, the activities were massive, the scene was warm, and the cultural atmosphere was strong.

According to reports, most of the worshippers were the well-known squire elders of four families. The day before the sacrificial ceremony, the leader who charges of this year's worship had already arranged the sacrificial hall through decorating the offering table with gorgeous satins and ribbons. On the day of sacrificial ceremony, all kinds of sacrifices, such as five animals, candy boxes, rice, soup, food and wine, were put on the offering table. The people who came to worship were dressed neatly and politely. They followed the direction of the chief worshipper with a solemn manner, and began to burn incense and paper in turn, then kneeled down to worship the ancestors.

With the changes of the times, the ancestral worship of Zhang clan has also experienced ups and downs. From the end of the Republic of China (1912-1949) to the first half century of reform and opening up, worship activities once entered a low ebb. In recent years, the ancestral worship activities have flourished with the prosperity of the country and the revival of traditional culture. Sacrificing ancestral hall and worshiping ancestors is a spontaneous activity of the masses, which reflects the moral custom, traditional habits and religious concepts of the Zhang clan. It is conducive to inherit the filial piety, knowledge and wisdom of the ancestors, and also places the ideal and hope of the whole clan. It enhances the unity and fraternity of the neighborhood, and plays a positive role in building a harmonious society and protecting folk culture.

In May 2014, Zhang Clan Ancestral Hall Worship Activities entered the fourth list of province-level intangible cultural heritage representative items.

Nine Folk Literature

Legend of Guan Zhong (province-level)

Guan Zhong, known as Guanzi, is an outstanding politician, philosopher, militarist and economist in China. His virtues, articles and contributions are outstanding and have been passed down through the ages. Guanzi ranks first among 40 Chinese cultural and historical figures, whose statue is located in the China Millennium Monument.

Fig 38 Guan Zhong's Statue

Scholars of all ages called Guanzi as the great pioneer and founder of Huai River civilization, and considered him a native of Yingshang county. According to Sima Qian's *Records of the Historian*, "Guan Zhong is a native of Yingshang." In Zhang Zhan[①]'s book, *Liezi Zhu* recorded that "Guan Zhong and Bao Shuya are all Yingshang people". According to

---

① "Zhang Zhan" was a philosopher of the Eastern Jin period (317–420).

archaeological research, "Yingshang" is not only an old place name in the Western Zhou Dynasty (1046 BC-771 BC), but also consistent with the geomorphological features of Guanguwan where Guan Zhong and Bao Shuya were born.

"Guanguwan" is now under the jurisdiction of Jianying village of Yingshang county. Each version of *Yingshang County Annals* records the geographical features, local conditions and customs of Guanguwan where Guan Zhong was born. It also records the legends of Guanzi Temple, Guan Zhong Stone, Sixian[1] Temple, Xiangxian[2] Temple and Guanzhong's Tomb which contains his personal effects. There is a cultural landscape near Guanguwan called "Wendi Chunfeng". This place is named according to the story of Confucius coming here for a visit. This place is also listed as one of the "eight scenic spots in Yingshang" historically. Guanzi was born 160 years earlier than Confucius. He is the ancestor of Confucius and is one of the founders of Qilu[3] Culture. It is reasonable for Confucius who advocated "respecting teachers and valuing education" went here for visiting Guanzi.

At the beginning, Guan Zhong was appointed as the tutor to Prince Jiu. Jiu and his brother Prince Xiaobai vied for the throne. Xiaobai won and became Duke Huan of Qi. Guan Zhong was imprisoned. Under Bao Shuya's recommendation, Duke Huan of Qi, regardless of his previous suspicions, appointed Guan Zhong as the chancellor. He lived up to the

---

[1] "Sixian" refers to people's honorific titles for famous people in a certain field.

[2] "Xiangxian" refers to people's honorific titles for famous people in a certain place.

[3] "Qilu" refers to the kingdoms of the Qi and Lu, in what is now Shandong, before the founding of the Qin Dynasty (221-207 BC). It is sometimes used as a name for Shandong province, one of the birthplaces of Chinese culture and civilization.

expectation, vigorously carried out political and fiscal reform in Qi. The capital was divided 21 districts: 15 of attendants, which provided the core of the Qi army and 6 of merchants, which provided the Qi state's trade revenue. The counties were grouped into five regions which were managed by officials at all levels. He set up the system of selecting talents that the scholars could get the assistance of chancellor after three times of examination and selection. Militarily, 5 households were formed into one Gui, and ten Guis as a Li. Four Lis formed a Lian, and ten Lians formed a district. Economically, all land was to be taxed according to its productivity. Forced labor shall be levied appropriately and plundering livestock was strictly forbidden. The government unified the coinage and its management, formulated the policy of fishing and salt boiling. Given this, the nation was rich and strong. On this basis, Guan Zhong helped Duke Huan of Qi to use "honor the king and drive off the barbarians" as a call to make allies with other states, making Duke Huan of Qi become the first leader of the vassal alliance in the Spring and Autumn Period. Therefore, Guanzi has the reputation of "the first chancellor in the world".

Guan Zhong was in business in his early years and became acquainted with Bao Shuya from his business. Later generations called their friendship as "David and Jonathan". Other legends, such as sharing money and property with each other like Guan Zhong and Bao Shuya, Guan Zhong and Bao Shuya were not become relatives, and an old hand is a good guide, have been widely spread in Yingshang county. During the Wanli reign (1573-1620) of the Ming Dynasty, Tu Long, the magistrate of Yingshang county and famous writer, built up "Guanbao Temple", erected stele and wrote articles to commemorate them. Their great friendship has been praised, admired and spread by later generations

"The legend of Guan Zhong" has a recorded history of nearly 200 years and has been handed down from generation to generation. Historians of Yingshang county such as Li Wenfa, Jing Canying, Feng Chuanli and Gong Wu have actively studied, demonstrated, written and published Guan Zhong's stories. Today, telling the good story about Guan Zhong has a very positive practical significance for inheriting and carrying forward his noble morality, humanistic thought and the idea of governing the country.

In July 2010, Legend of Guan Zhong entered the third list of province-level intangible cultural heritage representative items.

Chapter Two
State-level and Province-level
Representative Heritors of Intangible
Cultural Heritage Items

One Traditional Folk Art

Fuyang Paper-cut (state-level)

Cheng Xinghong (state−level) | related item: Fuyang Paper−cut

Cheng Xinghong was born in 1971, a native of Yingdong district of Fuyang city. He is an outstanding heritor of folk culture and the master of folk arts and crafts in Anhui province. Now, he is the director of the Chinese Paper-cut Art Committee, vice president of Fuyang Paper-cut Research Association, and chairman of Fuyang Cheng Style Paper-cut Culture and Art Co., Ltd.

He is the second-generation heritor of "Cheng Style Paper-cut" through inheriting his father Cheng Jianli, a master of Fuyang Paper-cut. Since childhood, he is fond of paper-cutting and has been deeply influenced and nurtured by his father. After diligent study and hard practice, he owned superb skills with a distinctive character of roughness without losing elegance. His purely handmade works are simple and generous without drawing samples. In his works, the big color block is flexible and changeable, and the lines are smooth. Most of themes of his works are about people, animals, flowers and birds, with strong storytelling and folk flavor characteristics.

His paper-cut works mainly include *Mouse Marrying*, *Children in the Water*, *The Silk Road* and so on. He has won many awards in exhibitions, competitions and folk arts and crafts expositions. He also went to Macao for folk cultural exchanges and participated in cultural exchanges between

China and foreign countries.

In June 2011, Cheng Xinghong entered the fourth list of state-level intangible cultural heritage representative heritors of Fuyang Paper-cut.

Zhu Kunying (province-level) | related item: Fuyang Paper-cut

Zhu Kunying was born in 1920 and died in 2008, a native of Fuyang city. He graduated from the Art Department of Anhui Normal University. He was the member of Anhui Branch of China Artists Association (now renamed as Anhui province Artists Association), and member of China Paper-cut Association.

Zhu Kunying has rich knowledge accumulation and high cultural and artistic quality. Over the past decades, with the love for nature and persistent pursuit of folk art, he has created a large number of elaborate paper-cut works with the themes of ancient and modern characters, auspicious animals, rare flowers under his skillful and simple techniques. His works are ingenious in shape, exquisite in cutting, and full of sense of life, which can express people's happy and festive feelings to the fullest. Whether simple, beautiful and natural colorful paper-cut works, or monochrome paper-cut works with smooth, sparse and delicate lines, all can exude a strong sense of local sentiment and a unique traditional folk style.

Zhu Kunying created thousands of art works which have abundant subjects and rich contents. These works include traditional Chinese painting, print and paper-cut. He participated in many provincial-level and state-level art exhibitions and won awards. His works had published in national professional newspapers for many times and had included in more than ten dictionaries of culture and art. As a teacher, he cultivated a large number of new paper-cut artists and made positive contributions to the transmission and development of Fuyang Paper-cut.

In May 2007, Zhu Kunying entered the first list of province-level intangible cultural heritage representative heritors of Fuyang Paper-cut.

Liu Jicheng (province-level) | related item: Fuyang Paper-cut

Liu Jicheng, pseudonym Shichuan (Chinese character: 石川), was born in 1943, a native of Taihe county, Anhui province. He is the member of China Artists Association and former vice president of China Paper-cut Association. He served as the chief editor for many books, such as *Chinese Contemporary Paper-cutters* and *Chinese Famous Paper-cut Artists*. In 2006, he was awarded the title of "the First Master of Arts and Crafts in Anhui province".

Liu Jicheng graduated from the Fine Arts Department of Anhui Academy of Arts. In his early years, he was engaged in painting, calligraphy and paper-cut, and later served as the leader of Fuyang folk art. Under his promotion, in the 1980s, Fuyang took the lead in setting up the "Paper-cut Research Association", the "Folk Art Research Office", journal of *Folk Art*, and the "China Paper-cut Research Association", which made positive contributions to the development of Fuyang Paper-cut as a national famous folk art brand.

In the theoretical research, Liu Jicheng has unique views on paper-cut. In the practice, he is skillful and consummate, and his representative works include *A Dream of Red Mansions*, *Kwan-yin Delivers Children*, *Brotherhood*, *Love and Education*, etc.

In May 2007, Liu Jicheng entered the first list of province-level intangible cultural heritage representative heritors of Fuyang Paper-cut.

Wu Qingping (province-level) | related item: Fuyang Paper-cut

Wu Qingping was born in 1971, a native of Fuyang city. She is the member of Chinese Folk Literature and Art Association and vice president of Fuyang Paper-cut Research Association.

Wu Qingping studied from Zhu Kunying and Cheng Jianli, two famous artists. On the basis of inheriting tradition, she constantly absorbed the essence of other folk paper-cut arts, innovated techniques, then forming her fresh, natural, lively, soft and exquisite artistic style. In 2007, she created the paper-cut scroll work, *Harmonious China* (cooperating with others). This work is 223 meters long and 1 meter wide, which was served as a gift for the 2008 Beijing Summer Olympics. CCTV and other media reported this event at that time. Her representative work *Beauties Wearing Flowers* won the prize in "Best Example Worldwide" Public Cultural Activities Exhibition held by the United Nations and was permanently collected.

In January 2011, Wu Qingping entered the third list of province-level intangible cultural heritage representative heritors of Fuyang Paper-cut.

Ge Tingyou (province-level) | related item: Fuyang Paper-cut

Ge Tingyou was born in 1968, a native of Fuyang city. He is the director of Chinese Paper-cut Art Committee, member of the Chinese Folk Literature and Art Association, and second master of Arts and Crafts in Anhui province.

Ge Tingyou fell in love with paper-cut when he was young, influenced by his mother's love on paper-cut and his grandfather's love on wood carving. Later, he studied with Jia Peixiu, a folk paper-cut artist from Jieshou city, and was taught by Liu Jicheng, a famous calligrapher and paper-cut artist in Fuyang city. He was diligent in learning and good at summarizing. Soon his art level rapidly raised. On the basis of absorbing the essence of Fuyang folk art, he integrated the spirit of the times into paper-cut, gradually forming the characteristics of naivety, simplicity, deepness, exaggeration and softness with strong local flavor.

Ge Tingyou has participated in many national exhibitions and won many prizes. In 2010, he was invited to the lecture called as "master's paper-cut lecture" held by the Shanghai World Expo. He was also awarded the title of "China's Top Ten Paper-cut Artists" by Chinese Paper-cut Art Committee and the honorary title of "Chinese Top Ten Paper-cutters" by the Organizing Committee of the Fifth National Paper-cut Competition. He had also been to South Korea and other countries and regions for folk cultural and artistic exchanges.

Over the years, Ge Tingyou has been devoted himself to the research and teaching of folk art in addition to paper-cut. He wrote many monographs, such as *Ballads of Paper-cut Techniques, Children's paper-*

cut, Paper-cut Textbooks of Senior University, Paper-cut Papers, Paper-cut Works, Fuyang Contemporary Folk Paper-cut and *Fuyang Folk Paper-cut Techniques*. He also serves as the visiting professor of College of Information Engineering of Fuyang Normal University, visiting professor of Huainan Normal University, and paper-cut teacher of Fuyang Elderly University.

In June 2011, Ge Tingyou entered the fourth list of province-level intangible cultural heritage representative heritors of Fuyang Paper-cut.

Ren Huaijian (province-level) | related item: Fuyang Paper-cut

Ren Huaijian was born in 1964, a native of Taihe county, Anhui province. He is the member of Chinese Paper-cut Art Committee, member of Anhui Folk Literature and Art Association, outstanding heritor of Anhui folk culture and master of folk arts and crafts.

Ren Huaijian learned from Wang Jiahe, a famous paper-cut artist. He absorbed many artistic elements from wood engraving, brick carving, New-Year pictures, architecture and operas. He also integrated the essence of Northern Chinese Paper-cut and Southern Chinese Paper-cut. With his exploration for the beauty of paper-cut, he gradually formed his own artistic characteristics, namely, novel imagination, full composition, rich layers, strong contrast, harmonious colors in black, white and gray, and bright rhythm. In terms of ornamentation, he appropriately uses the unique patterns of paper-cut such as zigzag pattern, crescent pattern, and jujube nucleus pattern, skillfully matches thick and thin lines with special patterns, making the works concise but not monotonous, rich but not trivial, airy and clear but not flamboyant and exaggerated, vivid but not unstable, with great decorative effect.

His main works include *Four Sons Studying Hard*, *The Jade Hall of Fortune Reflecting in Screen*, *Harmonious Coexistence*, *Admission of Five Sons*, *Four Seasons Vase*, *Eight Immortals Celebrating Longevity* and *Three Heroes Battling with Lu Bu*, etc. He has participated in many national exhibitions and won prizes.

In May 2019, Ren Huaijian entered the sixth list of province-level intangible cultural heritage representative heritors of Fuyang Paper-cut.

Huanggang Willow Weaving (state-level)

Wang Wenzhong (state-level) | related item: Huanggang Willow Weaving

Wang Wenzhong was born in 1962, a native of Funan county. He is a state-level heritor of willow weaving techniques, senior artisan in Anhui province, and outstanding craftsman of Huai River region. Now, he is the executive director of China Arts and Crafts Association and vice president of Fuyang Private Cultural Enterprises Association.

(Middle Figure is Wang Wenzhong)

Wang Wenzhong is especially fond of willow weaving techniques, and is good at learning, absorbing and using other techniques for reference. He is especially proficient in the core pingbian (two-dimensional weaving) technique of Huanggang Willow Weaving, and has brought this ordinary technique to a very high level. His works have both appearance and spirit, which are widely welcomed by users. Because these works integrate practicality, artistry and ornamentation. His main works include *Dragon-and-Tiger Bronze Ware*, *Seismograph*, *Twelve Zodiac Heads* and so on, which have been exhibited and awarded for many times. The products are also sold well at home and abroad.

In June 2011, Wang Wenzhong entered the fourth list of state-level intangible cultural heritage representative heritors of Huanggang Willow Weaving.

Sun Chuangui (province-level) | related item: Huanggang Willow Weaving

Sun Chuangui was born in 1962, a native of Funan county. He is the production manager and sample designer of Funan Jinyuan Willow Handicraft Co., Ltd.

Sun Chuangui is proficient in jingbian (knitting fabric with longitudinal warp loops) technique and has a high level of it. His works are exquisite and unique. He has won 32 patents such as "Research and Development of Heat-resistant and Environment-friendly Wicker Cup Holder" and "Rotary Craft Chair". His enterprise has won many honors such as "Provincial Specialized New Enterprise", "Provincial High-tech Cultivation Enterprise" and "Municipal High-quality Intellectual Property Cultivation Enterprise".

In 2010, his works *Bird's Nest*, *Vase* and *Photo Frame* were rated as excellent works by the Ministry of Culture and China Federation of Literary and Art Circles.

In March 2015, Sun Chuangui entered the fifth list of province-level intangible cultural heritage representative heritors of Huanggang Willow Weaving.

Du Style Copper Engraving (state-level)

Du Ping (state-level) | related item: Du Style Copper Engraving

Du Ping was born in 1960, a native of Yingdong district of Fuyang city. He is a Master of Arts and Crafts of Anhui province, vice chairman of Anhui Folk Art Association, and president of Anhui Du Style Copper Engraving Art Co., Ltd. He was awarded the third outstanding craftsman of Huai River region and other honorary titles.

Since childhood, under the instruction of his father, Du Ping has inherited this gradually disappearing ancient copper engraving technique and has been constantly exploring and innovating it. Technically, he learned from and absorbed the techniques of traditional cutting, inlay cutting and seal cutting, and used his own cutter. With white copper and brass as the main materials, beautiful patterns were engraved on the copper surface through multiple processes such as material selection, patterns confirming, engraving, polishing and baking. These processes eventually broadened the form of this traditional copper art, enriched its theme, and further improved the artistic expression. Given this, Du Style Copper Engraving can get a higher level.

Using knife as pen and copper as paper, Du Ping revived copper engraving, this traditional Chinese handicraft through his exquisite craftsmanship. His engraving objects are mostly famous for ink cartridge, paperweight, fumigation oven, teapot, wine vessel, plate, etc. The main themes of the patterns are characters, mountains and rivers, flowers and birds, which are full of scholarly style. His works have won many awards and have high cultural value and collection value.

In May 2018, Du Ping entered the fifth list of state-level intangible cultural heritage representative heritors of Du Style Copper Engraving.

Jieshou Embroidery (province-level)

Liu Lanying (province−level) | related item: Jieshou Embroidery

Liu Lanying was born in 1941, a native of Jieshou city, Anhui province. She is the province-level representative heritor of Jieshou Embroidery.

Liu Lanying learned from her mother Li Jinlan. Her embroidery is characterized by many stitch methods, including tioahua (stitch method that strictly accordance with the fabric warp and weft pattern), jiahua (one-side stitch), qianhua (two-sides stitch), duanmian xiuhua (stitch flowers on satin), butie xiuhua (stitch patterns on clothes). Her compositions are full of exaggerated shapes, vivid patterns and elegant colors. The main embroidery products include curtain, pillow case, apron, square handkerchief, insole, sock sole, belly binding, bed sheet, cover, door curtain, purse, embroidered pillow, embroidered shoes, collar, cuff, handbag, schoolbag and other daily necessities. The embroidery patterns mainly include figures, birds, scenery, animals, farming, hunting, dancing, entertainment, wedding, guard of honor, etc.

Her embroidery work *Goldfish Playing with Lotus* won the grand prize in the National Folk Arts Exhibition in 1984, and was praised by Zhang Ting, the dean of the Central Academy of Arts and Crafts (now renamed as Academy of Arts & Design of Tsinghua University), who praised it as "a unique work of art".

In January 2011, Liu Lanying entered the third list of province-level intangible cultural heritage representative heritors of Jieshou Embroidery.

Xiyang Embroidery (province-level)

Yuan Yuling (province-level) | related item: Xiyang Embroidery

Yuan Yuling was born in 1962, a native of Taihe county, Anhui province. She is the heritor of Fuyang outstanding folk culture and province-level folk craftsman.

Since childhood, Yuan Yuling learned embroidery from her mother, Yuan Songshi. Her needling technique combines the richness of Yue Embroidery, the delicacy of Shu Embroidery, the dignity of Jing Embroidery, the beauty and charm of Su Embroidery, and the ruggedness and simplicity of Bian Embroidery. Her embroidery works were well-received in the Sixth Chinese International Hui-Merchants Conference and Exhibition, and many of them were collected at home and abroad. In August 2010, she was invited to participate in the series activities of the First Chinese (held in Wangniudun town, Dongguan city) Double Seventh Culture Festival sponsored by Chinese Folk Literature and Art Association, and her selected work *Tiger-head-like Cap - the Sky of Wealth* won the bronze award; In 2011, her work *Cloud Shoulder* won the silver award at the Sixth China Folk Arts and Crafts Exposition; In 2012, his work *Lotus on Top of Tiger's Head* won the excellent award at China Folk Arts and Crafts Exposition; In 2014, the program, *Vernacular Culture* of CCTV-7 made a special report for her with the theme of "People's Good Craftsmanship in Fuyang".

In March 2015, Yuan Yuling entered the fifth list of province-level intangible cultural heritage representative heritors of Xiyang Embroidery.

Bai Li (province-level) | related item: Xiyang Embroidery

Bai Li was born in 1965, a native of Taihe county, Anhui province. She is the master of folk arts and crafts in Anhui province, director of the province intangible cultural heritage research association, director of Anhui Folk Literature and Art Association,  and director of Anhui Protection & Development Association for the Promotion of Traditional Arts & Crafts. Now, she is the general manager of Taihe Hongli Culture and Art Exchange Co., Ltd. and president of Taihe Embroidery Association.

Bai Li successively learned from Liu Lanying and Cai Meiying, two province-level famous embroidery masters. She absorbed the essence of Su Embroidery, then formed her own unique style. She used many stitch methods freely, such as knot stitch method, plain stitch method, inverted stitch method and loose stitch method. She has produced many works, such as tiger-head-like shoes, tiger-head-like cap, purse, cheongsam, Han clothing, characters, mountains and rivers, flowers and birds. These works are full of folk flavor and win many provincial awards in art exhibitions and competitions with high collection value. Among them, her representative works include *Portrait of Deng Xiaoping*, *Portrait of Xi Jinping*, *Leisure Autumn* and *Riverside Scene at the Pure Moon Festival*.

In May 2019, Bai Li entered the sixth list of province-level intangible cultural heritage representative heritors of Xiyang Embroidery

Two Traditional Opera

Huaibei Bnagzi Opera (state-level)

Wang Yonglan (state-level) | related item: Huaibei Bnagzi Opera

Wang Yonglan was born in 1963, a native of Fuyang city. She began to work in 1978. Now, she is the national first-grade actor, member of China Theatre Association and director of Anhui Theatre Association.

Wang Yonglan learned from Guo Jinfeng, Yang Zhizhong and Zheng Lianxin, three famous artists of Huaibei Bnagzi Opera. Under the training and education of these famous artists, she systematically studied the performance forms and singing skills of Huaibei Bangzi Opera, and organically combined dance with traditional performance forms. In terms of singing skills, she not only retains the high-pitched and simple characteristics of Huaibei Bangzi Opera, but also adds the characteristics of indirection and delicacy of prolonged tunes, gradually forming her own artistic style; In term of performance, she integrates traditional program forms and future makes some development and innovation. Her representative plays include the traditional plays such as *Butterfly Cup*, *Sisters Marrying Easily* and *Biography of Jigong*; the modern plays include *The Full Moon*, *Lives of Three Women* and *Nightmare*. She has participated in national, provincial and municipal major art activities for many times and has made outstanding achievements.

In May 2018, Wang Yonglan entered the fifth list of state-level intangible cultural heritage representative heritors of Huaibei Bnagzi Opera.

Jiang Xianglin (province−level) | related item: Huaibei Bnagzi Opera

Jiang Xianglin was born in 1962, a native of Bozhou city. He is the member of Chinese Theater Music Society, executive director of Anhui Opera Music Association, director of Anhui Theatre Association, national  second-grade performer and composer. Now, he is the deputy general manager of Fuyang Performing Arts Co., Ltd.

Jiang Xianglin learned from Wu Junxia, Zhu Shian and other famous veteran artists who passed away. He is familiar with the traditional performance forms of Huaibei Bangzi Opera as well as various plate-type structures of tuncs. After years of practice, he has been learning from and absorbing the techniques performed by these elder artists. In the tone and melody direction of Huaibei Bangzi Opera, he not only has retained the originally high-pitched, simple and generous characteristics, but also has developed delicacy in the high-pitched tunes. This highlights the local artistic features of Huaibei Bangzi Opera. He has won many awards in major provincial and municipal performances.

In January 2011, Jiang Xianglin entered the third list of province-level intangible cultural heritage representative heritors of Huaibei Bnagzi Opera.

Ma Bufeng (province–level) | related item: Huaibei Bnagzi Opera

Ma Bufeng was born in 1968, a native of Yingshang county, Anhui province. She is the national first-grade actor, member of China Theatre Association and member of Anhui Theatre Association. Now, she is the manager of Fuyang Bufeng Actor Service Co., Ltd.

Ma Bufeng learned from Guo Jinfeng, Zheng Lianxin, Yang Zhizhong and Xu ruoxuan, four famous artists. Her performance is exquisite, which can organically combine traditional and modern expression forms; Her tune is euphemistic and pleasant, forming her own unique artistic style. Her representative plays mainly include traditional plays such as *Sisters Marrying Easily* and *Bao Qingtian* and modern plays such as *Open Door Three Times*, *The lives of Three Women* and *Blooming Flowers and Full Moon*. She has participated in many provincial and municipal major performances and achieved outstanding results.

In March 2015, Ma Bufeng entered the fifth list of province-level intangible cultural heritage representative heritors of Huaibei Bnagzi Opera.

Funan Haizi Opera (state-level)

Xie Xuefang (province-level) | related item: Funan Haizi Opera

Xie Xuefang was born in 1954, a native of Funan county, Anhui province. She is a teacher of intangible cultural heritage training class in Funan county and representative heritor of Haizi Opera.

Since childhood, Xie Xuefang has been fond of singing Haizi Opera. In 1958, she was elected to the art troupe of Funan county, focusing on performing female in general and other main roles in more than 30 traditional and modern plays. She excavated and innovated more than ten sections of traditional singing tunes (including minor), and created more than thirty sections of new singing tunes. Her representative plays include *Beating Peach Blossom*, *Three High Fives*, *Tragedy of Dou'e*, *Rolling Bamboo Mat*, *The Red Lantern*, *The Red Detachment of Women*, *Spirit of Wangjiaba*, etc. With distinctive artistic features, these plays are deeply loved by the masses.

In November 2008, Xie Xuefang entered the second list of province-level intangible cultural heritage representative heritors of Funan Haizi Opera.

Li Yuying (province-level) | related item: Funan Haizi Opera

Li Yuying was born in 1945, a native of Funan county, Anhui province. He is a teacher of intangible cultural heritage training class in Funan county and a representative heritor of Haizi Opera.

Since childhood, Li Yuying studied from folk artists to sing Haizi Opera. Later, he began to participate in performance activities, and performed folk ditty, bass drum storytelling, allegro, etc., accumulating rich experience in folk art singing. In 1986, he engaged in directing and ballad creation work. Due to his hard learning, strong comprehension and newly creative ideas, he created and directed a number of excellent plays. In 2002, his directing work *Playing Lanterns* won the first prize in the National Small Plum Blossom Opera Competition; In 2011, his directing work *Special Bride* won the first director prize and the second performance prize in the Fifth Drama and Crosstalk Competition in Anhui province; In 2012, his directing work *Examiner* won the second prize of Haizi Opera Performance Competition held by the Department of Culture of Anhui province.

In November 2008, Li Yuying entered the second list of province-level intangible cultural heritage representative heritors of Funan Haizi Opera.

Sun Lixia (province-level) | related item: Funan Haizi Opera

Sun Lixia was born in 1943, a native of Funan county, Anhui province. She is an actor of art troupe of Funan county and teacher of Haizi Opera Art Inheritance Training School.

Sun Lixia was born in a family with rich artistic atmosphere. Her father is proficient in playing musical instruments and singing songs. Under the influence of her family, Sun Lixia loved folk literature and art since childhood, especially for Haizi Opera. In 1962, she was selected to the art troupe of Funan county. The characters she plays are beautiful and charming, which wins the hearts of the public. Her main representative plays include *Huaishu Village, Li Shuangshuang, Two Pieces of Flower Clothes*, etc.

In November 2008, Sun Lixia entered the second list of province-level intangible cultural heritage representative heritors of Funan Haizi Opera.

Dai Wanqing (province-level) | related item: Funan Haizi Opera

Dai Wanqing was born in 1943, a native of Funan county, Anhui province. He is the member of Anhui Theatre Association and tune class teacher in Haizi Opera Art Inheritance Training School.

In the 1960s, Wan Qing graduated from an art school of Funan county and was assigned to the art troupe to study art. He is good at performing the role of clown. He can play small figures vividly and dramatically. His representative works include *General Secretary's Coming to Wangjiaba*, *The Story of Forced Marriage*, *Standing Flower Wall*, *Shajiabang*, *Huaishu Village*, *One Millionth of a Second*, etc.

In March 2015, Dai Wanqing entered the fifth list of province-level intangible cultural heritage representative heritors of Funan Haizi Opera.

Yingshang Tui Opera (province-level)

Cao Shuzhi (province-level) | related item: Yingshang Tui Opera

Cao Shuzhi, stage name: "Xiaoerjie" in Chinese, was born in 1934, a native of Yingshang county. He is a famous performer of Tui Opera in Huai River basin.

Cao Shuzhi loved folk art in his life and devoted himself to the development of Tui Opera for decades. With skillful and rich performing techniques, he crated many living and artistic stage images of Tui Opera. More importantly, he also attached great importance to the inheritance and innovation of Tui Opera, and played an irreplaceable role in protecting four-sentence Tui Opera of Yingshang county.

The plays he created, adapted and performed are humorous in content with unity of form and spirit. Such plays *Sending Fragrant Tea, Saving Mother by Cutting Liver, Zhu Baishen Repudiating His Wife, Travelingl around West Lake, Repudiating Wife Dingxiang, Big Lady's House* can display the daily life and customs of the people who are living in Huai River basin, which leave a deep impression on the audience and have a great influence in the local area.

In November 2008, Cao Shuzhi entered the second list of province-level intangible cultural heritage representative heritors of Yingshang Tui Opera.

Three Traditional Folk Music

Huai River Gong-drum (province-level)

Zhu Zhanyong (province–level) | related item: Huai River Gong–drum

Zhu Zhanyong was born in 1952, a native of Zhutai village, Lukou town, Yingshang county. His hometown has a long history of playing gongs and drums. He grew up along with the sound of Huai River gong-drum and has been engaged in this artistic career.

Since 1968, Zhu Zhanyong began his performance career with Huai River Gong-drum. He became an artist for decades and never left the stage. He is a versatile performer who can play both gongs and drums in the traditional folk gong-drum performances. The drums and gongs he played are clear in sound. When he is performing, the sound can be swift as strong wind and heavy rain, and it also can be slow as gentle flowing water. He also organically integrates the single performance of gongs and drums into the accompaniment of flower-drum lanterns dance, which makes these elements combined well. He can dance while singing and also sing while beating, which is very popular among the local people.

In January 2011, Zhu Zhanyong entered the third list of province-level intangible cultural heritage representative heritors of Huai River Gong-drum.

Fentai Suona (province-level)

Wang Feilong (province-level) | related item: Fentai Suona

Wang Feilong was born in 1986, a native of Fentai town, Taihe county, Anhui province. He is the executive director of Northern Anhui Suona Association, representative heritor of Fentai Suona.

In his early years, Wang Feilong learned from his father Wang Jinyu, a suona artist, for learning local suona playing techniques. After finishing his studies, he went to other places in Henan province and Anhui province in order to learn from other artists and study their advantages. He inherited and developed his father's suona playing skills and formed his own artistic characteristics.

Through continuous practice, absorption and innovation, Wang Feilong fully performs the singing skills of suona, such as slide sound and swallow sound. His suona sound is loud, graceful, high-pitched, varied and rich in connotation. He can also freely use suona to play local operas such as Bangzi Opera, Flower-drum Opera, Liuqin Opera. He can also use suona sound to vividly show the characters of different roles in operas, which has certain appeal and is well-received by the local people.

In May 2019, Wang Feilong entered the sixth list of province-level intangible cultural heritage representative heritors of Fentai Suona.

Four Traditional Sports, Entertainment and Aerobatics

Linquan Aerobatics (province-level)

Hou Deshan (province-level) | related item: Linquan Aerobatics

Hou Deshan was born in 1923, a native of Mo county (now renamed as Weihui city) of Henan province, and died in 2017. He is an acrobatic artist, member of China Acrobats Association, director of Anhui Acrobats Association, and founder of Yingxian Circus of Linquan county.

When 12 years old, Hou Deshan was attracted by the wonderful acrobatic performance of the acrobatics troupe of Xuzhou city. He began to learn aerobatics with the troupe and regarded this art as his lifelong pursuit. In the 1960s, Hou Deshan immigrated from Henan province to Xiaoli village of Yingxian town, Linquan county, where he took root and began to train acrobats. He was good at learning from, absorbing and summarizing acrobatic techniques, then innovated and developed the acrobatic art of Linquan county. He was especially good at performing skillful programs such as *Five Beans Flying Together* and *Through the Sword Mountain*. Among these programs, *Fire Spraying* is his masterpiece. He can freely spray "fire mushroom", "double-headed fire", "fireball", "fire fork", "fire snake" (6 meters high), "fireball in and out", "fire double-whip" and other shapes from his mouth. His unique skill was well-known throughout the country and he was known as the "god of fire".

The Yingxian Circus founded by Hou Deshan is full of talents. These wonderful performances have not only been praised by the audience, but also attracted the attention of the movie and television circles. In 1987, he was invited to take part in the shooting of colorful feature film *Red Revenge* and *The Great Xiangguo Temple* made by Beijing Film Academy; In 1988, his team cooperated with Kaifeng city to shoot the TV series *The Emperor Plays Polo*; In 2000, Hong Kong TV station took Hou Deshan as the prototype to shoot the TV series *Stories of Chinese Folk Artists*. More than 30 newspapers and magazines including *People's Daily Overseas Edition*, *Ta Kung Pao* and *Ming Pao*, have reported on the grand performances of Hou Deshan and his Yingxian Circus.

In November 2008, Hou Deshan entered the second list of province-level intangible cultural heritage representative heritors of Linquan Aerobatics.

Hou Zhongyi (province–level) | related item: Linquan Aerobatics

Hou Zhongyi was born in 1957, a native of Henan province. He is the member of China Acrobats Association, second-generation heritor of Hou-family Troupe of Linquan Acrobatic Circus, and legal representative of Linquan Yingxian Zhongyi Circus Performance Co., Ltd.

Hou Zhongyi learned from Cheng Lianbao, a famous acrobatic artist, and carried forward "Cheng Style Great Martial Art". In 1987, Hou Zhongyi led his troupe to take part in the shooting of the large-scale colorful feature film *Red Revenge* and *Golden Dart Hero*; In 2014, he took part in the shooting of the film *The Soul of Art* which took acrobatics as the theme. At the first to the fourth provincial Folk Acrobatic Arts Festivals, his troupe won many awards. He also led the team to visit and perform in Cairo, Thailand and Sweden on behalf of Department of Culture of Anhui province three times, and carried out acrobatic cultural exchange activities between China and foreign countries, winning honors for the homeland.

In June 2011, Hou Zhongyi entered the fourth list of province-level intangible cultural heritage representative heritors of Linquan Aerobatics.

Yin Yanchun (province-level) | related item: Linquan Aerobatics

Yin Yanchun was born in 1947, a native of Linquan county, Anhui province. He is the member of China Acrobats Association and former vice chairman of Anhui Acrobats Association.

Yin Yanchun has been engaged in acrobatics for more than 50 years and has made positive contributions to the inheritance, development and innovation of local acrobatics and magic. IIe founded two acrobatic training bases. He has been persisting in guiding young actors to practice, rehearse traditional programs and compile innovative programs for a long time. He has trained more than 400 acrobatic and magic artists.

Yin Yanchun has eight acrobatic performance troupes. Among these troupes, Linquan Feiyan Acrobatic Troupe, Linquan Yintong Acrobatic Troupe and Linquan Feitian Acrobatic Troupe, are rated into top 100 troupes of Anhui province. In 2012, his troupes were selected into top 100 cultural enterprises of Anhui province. His acrobatic troupes have been active in Guangdong city, Shanghai city and Wuhan city all year round. In 2018 alone, these troupes performed 2860 times, including nearly 100 public welfare performances. In the same year, a troupe composed of 12 people led by his daughter Yin Hong went to Hong Kong for 20 performances. The representative works include traditional programs such as *Immortal Picking Beans*, *Seven-section Bottle*, *Mandarin Ducks Stick*, *Chinese Ring*, *The Shaking Board*, and *Moving Objects in Space* and innovative programs such as *The Soul of the Army*, *Magic Love*, *The Eagle Spreads Its Wings*, *Young Jiang Ziya* and *Ballet on the Shoulder*. From 2009 to 2017, his troupes had participated in the provincial Folk Acrobatic Art

Festivals four times and won first prize five times; In 2012, his innovative magic program *Magic Love* won won the gold award in the third "golden cane" magic conference in the Yangtze River Delta region; From 2016 to 2017, he participated in cultural exchange activities organized by Department of Culture of Anhui province in Egypt and Sweden.

In November 2008, Yin Yanchun entered the second list of province-level intangible cultural heritage representative heritors of Linquan Aerobatics.

Tongcheng Fire Fork and Fire Whip (province-level)

He Shunli (province-level) | related item: Tongcheng Fire Fork and Fire Whip

He Shunli was born in 1953, a native of Tongcheng town of Linquan county, Anhui province. He is a famous performer of Tongcheng Fire Fork and Fire Whip, known as an "master of fire whip".

He Shunli began to learn this art at the age of 17 with Ma Shanliang as his teacher. Due to his diligence, he soon mastered the performing skills of fire fork and fire whip, as well as the local folk arts such as Lion Dance, Dragon Dance, Stilt and Stubborn Donkey Gait. His performance is full of emotion and joy. When he is performing, the sparks from forks or whips are splashing and dazzling with beautiful lines in the air. Such circles are connected to extend various figures. Under the background of percussion music, his performances add some elements and moves of Yangko Dance, which are very wonderful. These programs include *Single Jump, Crossing Pear Blossom, Holding Fire in Arms, Carrying Fire at Night, Playing Alone in Daytime, Red on the Back of the Big Cross, King Unloading Armor, Zhang Fei's Horse Riding,* and *Eighteen Rolls on the Ground,* etc.

He Shunli also attached importance to the inheritance of Linquan Fire Fork and Fire Whip. Over the past 20 years, he has cultivated a group of newcomers with his teacher Ma Shanxin and others. Whenever there are holidays, temple fairs and celebrations, he will lead his team to perform fire forks and fire whip. From 2009 to 2017, his team had participated in the opening ceremony performance of Folk Acrobatic Art Festival of Anhui province four times and received high praise.

In January 2011, He Shunli entered the third list of province-level intangible cultural heritage representative heritors of Tongcheng Fire Fork and Fire Whip.

Wuyin Bagua Boxing (province-level)

Ma Jusen (province-level) | related item: Wuyin Bagua Boxing

Ma jusen was born in 1963, a native of Funan county, Anhui province. Now, he is the president of Wuyin Bagua Boxing Research Association of Funan county.

Since childhood, Ma Jusen loved martial arts and was taught by Ma Hanqing, the famous heritor of Wuyin Bagua Boxing. He practiced hard with high understanding on martial art. He mastered the basic routine of Wuyin Bagua Boxing and other fighting equipment routines. His boxing skills are as rigid and flexible as a rock, or as light as a goose feather, or as fast as an ape. He has participated in many competitions and won 4 gold medals and 2 silver medals in Fuyang Traditional Martial Arts Competition.

In March 2015, Ma Jusen entered the fifth list of province-level intangible cultural heritage representative heritors of Wuyin Bagua Boxing.

Taihe Wudang Tai Chi (province-level)

Yang Chun (province−level) | related item: Taihe Wudang Tai Chi

Yang Chun, Taoist monastic name: Jianyunzi (Chinese character: 鉴云子), was born in 1964, a native of Taihe county, Anhui province. He is the fourteenth-generation heritor of Taihe Wudang Tai Chi, ranks seventh section in Chinese martial arts and serves as one of Top 100 in Wudang. Now, he is a senior coach of Fuyang Wushu Team.

As a child, Yang Chun practiced Waijia Boxing and Wudang Kungfu with Fan Ruitu, a famous master of folk martial arts. Later, he got the direct teaching of Wudang Tai Chi by Zhang Xingzhou, a famous master. He not only has a solid foundation of martial arts of the physical education, but also has a profound understanding and unique insight of internal training and legal theory, gradually forming his own unique style. On behalf of Anhui province, he has successively participated in the third, fourth and fifth World Traditional Wushu Championships and the Eighth Shanghai International Wushu Exposition. With his excellent martial arts, he has won the group D champion of Taihe Wudang Tai Chi and the excellent performance award.

Yang Chun has been practicing martial arts for more than 40 years. He has been engaged in martial arts training and traditional martial arts research for more than 30 years. He has compiled many books such as *Taoist True Wudang Ancestor Zhang Tai Chi* and published many papers in *Wudang* and *Chinese Martial Arts*. In recent years, he has devoted himself to promoting and popularizing Wudang martial arts and spreading Tai Chi

Culture widely, with more and more scholars following him. The students at home and abroad who have been tutored and instructed by him have won gold and silver models in martial arts competitions for many times, making positive contributions to the promotion of Chinese martial arts.

In May 2019, Yang Chun entered the sixth list of province-level intangible cultural heritage representative heritors of Taihe Wudang Tai Chi.

Five Traditional Dance

Yingshang Flower-drum Lantern Dance (state-level)

Wang Chuanxian (state-level) | related item: Yingshang Flower-drum Lantern Dance

Wang Chuanxian, art name: Zi' an (Chinese character: 子安), stage name: "yitaiosheng"(means he is very thin like a rope), also known as "xiaomifeng" (means he likes a bee when performing), was born in 1923 and died in 2010, a native of Lukou town, Yingshang county. In 1990, he won the honorary title of "top ten veteran artists of Flower-drum Lantern Dance in Anhui province".

Wang Chuanxian was good at performing the role of female in general because of his slim figure, good voice and feminine makeup appearance. He was also good at playing folk gong-drums. He was a good actor who was deeply loved by the audience. In the "big flower scene" directed or performed by him, there are more than 20 dance formations such as "two dragons coming out of the water", "dragon wagging its tail", "snake molts", "moving around the fence", "walk through four doors", "five gates", "three lead fields", "piling flowers" and "unloading flowers". Especially in the "moving around the fence" formation, it can turn to other new dance forms, such as "long fence", "group fence", "double door rotor", "single door rotor" with unique styles. Wang Chuanxian was also good at performing in "small flower scene". When performing, he would act the role of female in general to dance solo or matching with drum to dance. He would hold a handkerchief in one hand and a folding fan in the other, performing various moves, footwork, posture and skills. The melody was elegant, the dancing posture was beautiful, and the singing was euphemistic.

He also creatively incorporated acrobatics and martial arts performance skills into Flower-drum Lantern Dance, and made various beautiful shapes on the stage. His representative works include traditional plays such as *Small Cattle, Attacking Xuzhou, Sending Husband to Govern the Huai River*, and *Sighing at the Fifth Night* and modern plays *March Third*, which have become the classics of Yingshang Flower-drum Lantern Dance and have been well-received by the masses.

In February 2008, Wang Chuanxian entered the second list of state-level intangible cultural heritage representative heritors of Yingshang Flower-drum Lantern Dance.

Chen Yuhua (state-level) | related item: Yingshang Flower-drum Lantern Dance

Chen Yuhua was born in 1949, a native of Shencheng town, Yingshang county. She is a folk artist of Flower-drum Lantern Dance.

At the age of 13, she learned from Zhang Xiaoshun, a famous artist of Flower-drum Lantern Dance. Later, she learned from Jiang Maoxuan (stage name: Jiang Duizi), another veteran artist. She gradually grew into a distinctive folk dance performance artist. In the process of performing Flower-drum Lantern Dance, Chen Yuhua absorbed the characteristics of female role in Chinese opera, and integrated its performance advantages of hands, eyes, body method and footwork into Flower-drum Lantern Dance. Her most outstanding artistic feature is that she is good at using flower fans. By innovating and skillfully using holding fan, kneading fan and backing fan these forms, she combines more than 40 kinds of fan flower performance techniques such as "chop", "shake", "bump", "throw", "knead", "pull", "cast", "cover", "clutch" with other emotional movements to in order to show exquisite performance. By doing this, Yingshang Flower-drum Lantern Dance is more wonderful and attractive, and also increases the warm and joyful mood.

At the same time, in the dance performance which varies from person to person, from place to place and from time to time, she incisively and organically combines the improvisation and flexibility of Yingshang Flower-drum Lantern Dance, which positively promotes the development of this art.

In May 2018, Chen Yuhua entered the fifth list of state-level intangible cultural heritage representative heritors of Yingshang Flower-drum Lantern Dance.

Yang Dianhuan (province-level) | related item: Yingshang Flower-drum Lantern Dance

Yang Dianhuan was born in 1947, a native of Yanghu town, Yingshang county. He is a famous performing artist of Yingshang Flower-drum Lantern Dance.

Since childhood, Yang Dianhuan loved the Flower-drum Lantern Dance. In 1958, he learned from Tang Huiyun (a student of Tang Peijin, a master of Yingshang Flower-drum Lantern Dance) to learn how to perform the role of female in general. When performing, Yang Dianhuan used skillful moves, with flexible, fluent, natural and unrestrained posture. He timely integrated the symbolic postures into the performance of Flower-Drum Lantern Dance. These postures include "a single-door rotor", "a thousand-hand avalokitesvara", "two dragons spitting whiskers", "snake molts", "piling flowers and unloading flowers", "phoenix nodding three times", "double fences" and so on. He paid special attention to the unique moves of female in general. These moves included "uphill step", "cross step", "well-proportioned step", "cloud step", "little girl's step", "wind swinging willow step", "magpie making wind step", "turning-over step", etc. At the same time, he combined with the using-fan techniques of "throwing fan", "turning fan", "holding fan", "pulling fan", "sunshade fan" and so on. Given these, the audience could enjoy the art in the complex changing movement.

In March 2015, Yang Dianhuan entered the second list of province-level intangible cultural heritage representative heritors of Yingshang Flower-drum Lantern Dance.

Taihe Lion Lantern Dance (province-level)

Xue Cheng (province-level) | related item: Taihe Lion Lantern Dance

Xue Cheng was born in 1990, a native of Taihe county, Anhui province. He is the sixth-generation heritor of Taihe Lion Lantern Dance and president of Taihe Yiheng Dragon and Lion Dance Club.

Since childhood, Xue Cheng learned lion dance from his father. With his talent and constant practice, he soon mastered the essentials of lion dance and gradually formed his own artistic characteristics. His performance combines the dance characteristics of the lion dance schools of the Southern and Northern China. Accompanied by the sound of gongs and drums and fireworks, the performance is grand, high-spirited with a strong sense of rhythm. His performance shows the beast and spirit of the lion to the fullest, which is well-received by the audience.

For more than 20 years, Xue Cheng has been engaged in the inheritance of Lion Lantern Dance while performing. In 2010, he founded Taihe Yiheng Dragon and Lion Dance Club. In 2016, this club entered the school and founded "interest-oriented class of lion lantern dance" that taught dragon dance and lion dance skills, which promoted the development and spread of Taihe Lion Lantern Dance.

In May 2019, Xue Cheng entered the sixth list of province-level intangible cultural heritage representative heritors of Taihe Lion Lantern Dance.

Six Traditional Craftsmanship

Jieshou Painted Pottery (state-level)

Lu Qunshan (state-level) | related item: Jieshou Painted Pottery

Lu Qunshan was born in 1950, a native of Tianying town, Jieshou city. He is the member of Chinese Folk Literature and Art Association, member of China Arts and Crafts Association, director of Anhui Arts and Crafts Association, master of provincial folk crafts and general manager of Jieshou Lu Style Carved Painted Pottery Co., Ltd.

Lu Qunshan studied with his father Lu Shanyi (a master of Chinese arts and crafts) for the craftsmanship of pottery when he was young. Under the guidance of his father, he made rapid progress. He has made a bold process adjustment in terms of the shaping, glazing color, and firing temperature of the pottery products. Series works in tall and slender shape made by "daomaren" technique can be viewed his representative works. His works are accompanied by green water-ripple glaze, which have been praised by experts and other people. Collected by many museums, his works have won many national and provincial awards and exported to a dozen countries and regions. In 2011, his painted pottery *General Jar* won the "tenth Chinese folk literature and arts award".

In June 2007, Lu Qunshan entered the first list of state-level intangible cultural heritage representative heritors of Jieshou Painted Pottery.

Wang Jingsheng (state-level) | related item: Jieshou Painted Pottery

Wang Jingsheng was born in 1944, a native of Jieshou county, Anhui province. He is the director of Anhui Arts and Crafts Association, member of Anhui Folk Artists Association and master of province-level folk crafts. Now, he is the general manager of Jieshou Jingsheng Painted Pottery Co., Ltd.

Wang Jingsheng learned from Han Meilin, a master of painted pottery. He is proficient in the pottery production processes such as clay shaping, clay repairing, patterns carving, glazing and firing. He makes great innovations on Jieshou Painted Pottery. Equipping the pottery with the top cover and the base makes, he makes the overall image of the painted pottery rich in three-dimensional effect and the glaze texture. Therefore, these potteries are widely welcomed. In 2015, his representative work, the extra-large *"Tri-color Carved Vase"*, won the *"*national hundred flowers award*"*.

In June 2007, Wang Jingsheng entered the first list of state-level intangible cultural heritage representative heritors of Jieshou Painted Pottery.

Lu Lihua (province–level) | related item: Jieshou Painted Pottery

Lu Lihua was born in 1965, a native of Tianying town of Jieshou county, Anhui province. She is the member of the Chinese Folk Literature and Art Association, member of Anhui Artists Association, and first-batch arts and crafts artists of Anhui province.

Since childhood, Lu Lihua was influenced by ancestral pottery portrayal art. Then she studied with his father Lu Shanyi to inherit the pottery production techniques. She fully mastered the special engraving technique of distinctive "daomaren" technique produced by his father, especially proficient in engraving patterns under the tread glaze of painted pottery. She was good at engraving patterns by bamboo stick and steel stylus. And the patterns she engraved is life-like, vivid and expressive with powerful, vivid, smooth and natural lines.

On the basis of inheriting the traditional style, Lu Lihua has broken new ground on painted pottery. Her series works, *Daomaren Carving Jar* were sold at home and abroad, which were also collected by many famous artists. In 2004, the painted pottery *Three Heroes Battling with Lu Bu* won the excellence award of the First Chinese Folk Crafts Fair. In 2008, she participated in the final of the 4th National Ceramic Vocational Skills Competition and won the title of "technical expert".

In November 2008, Lu Lihua entered the second list of province-level intangible cultural heritage representative heritors of Jieshou Painted Pottery.

Lu Hua (province-level) | related item: Jieshou Painted Pottery

Lu Hua was born in 1962, a native of Jieshou city, Anhui province. Now, he is the artistic director and chief ceramic craftsman of Anhui Huiban Arts and Crafts Development Co., Ltd.

When he was young, Lu Hua learned painted pottery production techniques from his father Lu Shanyi. His works are mainly colored pottery, which can be used as altars, pots, boxes, vases and so on. His works are characterized by uniform thickness of the pottery body and beautiful shape. He also innovated the hollowing technology, which makes the work full of strong three-dimensional effect. In 2007, *The Tri-color Wine Jar* he made won the gold award in Anhui Arts and Crafts Exhibition.

In January 2011, Lu Hua entered the third list of province-level intangible cultural heritage representative heritors of Jieshou Painted Pottery.

Chen Cuiying (province–level) | related item: Jieshou Painted Pottery

Chen Cuiying was born in 1952, a native of Jieshou city, Anhui province. She is a province-level representative heritor of Jieshou Painted Pottery.

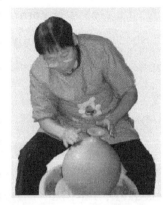

Learning from a master named Han Meilin, Chen Cuiying was proficient in clay shaping, clay repairing, patterns carving, glazing and firing pottery. Most of her works are depictions of flowers, birds, insects, and fish, with delicate brushwork, smooth lines, rounded composition, and simple patterns.

In 2007, *Long–neck Carved Vase* and *Bogu Vase* jointly produced by Chen Cuiying and Wang Jingsheng, a state-level heritor of painted pottery, were exhibited at the 7th China (held in Shenzhen city) International Cultural Industry Expo, winning the silver award of Chinese Arts and Crafts Cultural Creativity Award.

In March 2015, Chen Cuiying entered the fifth list of province-level intangible cultural heritage representative heritors of Jieshou Painted Pottery.

Zhang Qianwen (province-level) | related item: Jieshou Painted Pottery

Zhang Qianwen was born in 1985, a native of Jieshou city, Anhui province. She is a national first-grade artist, senior artist, master of Chinese traditional crafts, member of China Arts and Crafts Association, and member of the Anhui Folk Literature and Art Association.

Zhan Qianwen studied from Lu Shanyi, a master of Chinese arts and crafts, and Lu Qunshan, another master of Chinese ceramic arts. She is mostly proficient in engraving techniques of painted pottery. Her works are mainly composed of "daomaren" series and some characters from historical stories. Her works are full of straightforward and powerful lines, fruity and decent layout. The characters are vivid and warhorses are lifelike, which reflect the organic combination of modern and traditional styles and the primitive simplicity of pottery. People can feel the fine tradition of Anhui-style ancient prints from her works.

In 2007, her painted pottery work, *Daomarem Three-color Carved Parterre and Guanyin Vase* won the gold award in the Anhui Arts and Crafts Competition.

In March 2015, Zhang Qianwen entered the fifth list of province-level intangible cultural heritage representative heritors of Jieshou Painted Pottery.

Linquan Brush (province-level)

Cao Ruzhang (province-level) | related item: Linquan Brush

Cao Ruzhang was born in 1982 and died in 2011, a native of Tanpeng town of Linquan county, Anhui province. He is a master of Arts and Crafts of Anhui province.

At the age of 14, he began his long and hard brush-making career through learning from Li Wanzhong, a brush-making master in the Qing Dynasty. Under the true instruction of the master and his own careful study, his brush-making techniques became more and more consummate. Finally, he became a master in this art, which also laid a foundation for the development and prosperity of Linquan Brush.

In 1950, Cao Ruzhang began to take up the research and production of brush in Tanpeng town. Later, he was appointed as the director of Brush Production Cooperative in Yangqiao town. During the "Great Cultural Revolution" (1966-1976), he was labeled as a bad example of "taking the road of capitalism" because of brush making. After the Third Plenary Session of the Eleventh Central Committee (1978), he returned to this career again with vitality and energy. In 1982, he set up "Wendetang" Brush Company operated by his family in Tanpeng town. The brushes he made which were called "eight pillar optimus" won the first prize at the National Township Enterprise Product Fair. In 1992, he elaborately produced a brush called "prosperity" to contribute to Comrade Deng Xiaoping. This brush is collected in the National Museum of China now. In the year of Hong Kong's return (1997), the special 1.997-meter-high brush was presented to the former Hong Kong chief executive Tung Chee Hwa, which was specially commended by the Hong Kong Special Administrative Region. In 1998, he made a special brush which was selected as a souvenir for former U.S. President Clinton's visit to China, which promoted friendly international exchanges. He was also awarded the honorary titles of "the first province-level master of arts and crafts" and the annual "China's hundred industrial celebrities and caring figures".

In January 2011, Cao Ruzhang entered the third list of province-level intangible cultural heritage representative heritors of Linquan Brush.

Zhang Xiuyao (province–level) | related item: Linquan Brush

Zhang Xiuyao was born in 1952, a native of Tanpeng town of Linquan county, Anhui province. He is the member of the Anhui Folk Literature and Art Association, master of arts and crafts in Anhui province and deputy of the 2nd and 3rd People's Congress of Fuyang city.

At the age of 15, Zhang Xiuyao started to learn brush making technique, and got the instruction of his father Zhang Linde, a master of brush making and calligrapher. In 1977, he assisted his father to establish "Lintan Brush Shop". Zhang Xiuyao innovated boldly based on the traditional brush-making craftsmanship. He created more than 100 new craft brushes and a variety of high-, middle- and low-end gift brush sets, including goat's-hair brush, wolf's-hair brush, brownish rabbit's-hair brush, and brush made of two or more kinds of animal hair. Among them, the brush called "kowloon playing with ink", jointly created with his father won the gold prize in China Patent Technology Products Exposition in 1995 for the unique patented technology and excellent artistic effect of painting and calligraphy. Based on the only existing brush from Tang Dynasty (618-907) which was brought to Japan by Monk Jianzhen in that period, he imitated and developed a kind of brush which is highly similar with the original. This also filled blank in the production of this brush in China and made traditional Linquan Brush shining with brilliance.

In January 2011, Zhang Xiuyao entered the third list of province-level intangible cultural heritage representative heritors of Linquan Brush.

Cao Dianming (province-level) | related item: Linquan Brush

Cao Dianming was born in 1967, a native of Tanpeng town of Linquan county, Anhui province. He is the master of arts and crafts in Anhui province, president of Fuyang Brush Industry Association, curator of Fuyang Wendetang Art Museum, and legal representative of Anhui Wendetang Cultural Communication Co., Ltd.

Inheriting from his father's pen-making techniques, Cao Dianming innovated the techniques and produced many brushes which were sent to participate in state-level and province-level exhibitions and performances of intangible cultural heritage for many times. His works also won many honorary titles, such as "famous and high-quality products in Anhui province", "Anhui famous brand" and "Anhui time-honored brand". In 1985, brush created by Wendetang Brush Shop won the first prize in the National township Enterprise Product Trade Fair. In 1992, his company created a special brush as a gift sent to Comrade Deng Xiaoping. This brush is now in the National Museum of China as a permanent collection.

In March 2015, Cao Dianming entered the fifth list of province-level intangible cultural heritage representative heritors of Linquan Brush.

Zhao Bin (province–level) | related item: Linquan Brush

Cao Dianming was born in 1962, a native of Tanpeng town, Linquan county. He is the master of arts and crafts in Anhui province and chairman of Linquan Longbi Brush Industry Co., Ltd.

At the age of 18, Zhao Bin began to learn to make brushes. Under the careful guidance of Cao Ruzhang, a master of brush making and his own efforts, he soon grasped the brush production processes and continued to innovated these processes constantly. Then, he formed his unique style featured in ingenious conception, gorgeous and decent workmanship. Later, he founded his brands which were called as "Jiang Shang Brush" and "Bei Brush".

In 2011, Zhao Bin built "Linquan Brush Museum" so as to attract calligraphers nationwide to come here for communication and to make more people realize Linquan Brush. In 2014, his self-developed "screen hanging brush" won the gold medal at the First China (held in Hefei city) Intangible Cultural Heritage Exhibition. At the same year, his work also won the gold medal of Anhui Arts and Crafts Association. In 2016, his self-developed two patents which were called as "eight pillar optimus multifunctional brush" and "screen hanging brush holder" got the authorization and patent certificates issued by the China National Intellectual Property Administration.

In May 2019, Zhao Bin entered the sixth list of province-level intangible cultural heritage representative heritors of Linquan Brush.

Zuisan Qiu Liquor Traditional Brewing (province-level)

Yang Hongwen (province-level) | related item: Zuisan Qiu Liquor Traditional Brewing

Yang Hongwen was born in 1970, a native of Fuyang city. As a national first-level (senior) technician and senior engineer, he enjoys the special allowance of the State Council. He was awarded the title of "the 12th state-level  technical expert", "state-level expert in youth group" and "state-level technical expert of brewing industry". Moreover, he was awarded the "national liquor judge" qualification certificate for two consecutive sessions and passed the "national liquor taster" professional certification. Now, he is the chief engineer of Golden Seed Winery Co., Ltd and dean of the Golden Seed Winery Health Quality Research Institute of Jiangnan University.

After graduating from university in 1992, Yang Hongwen devoted himself into the liquor brewing industry. Through the organic combination of bioengineering techniques and traditional brewing techniques, he had increased the production rate of Qu liquor by 20 percent. A series of liquor brands such as "Golden Seeds", "Seed Liquor" and "Zuishan Qiu Liquor" that were researched and developed by Yang Hongwen simultaneously passed the "green food" certification issued by China Green Food Development Center, making Golden Seed Winery Co., Ltd rank first in liquor industry of Anhui province. He also pioneered the physical "constant cellar temperature" process. With the concept of "healthy and refreshing liquor" as the guide, the idea of "green, healthy, low-carbon and fashionable" was integrated into the research and production of liquor, which breaks through the tradition of liquor aroma determining the type of liquor. The "soft liquor" formulated by him was recognized as the local standard of Anhui province. In the final of the Second National Liquor Tasting Professional Skills Competition, Yang Hongwen won the title of "state-level technical expert of brewing industry" with the first place of Anhui province.

In March 2015, Yang Hongwen entered the fifth list of province-level intangible cultural heritage representative heritors of Zuisan Qiu Liquor Traditional Brewing.

Jinyu Wan Liquor Brewing (province-level)

Duan Zhaofa (province–level) | related item: Jinyu Wan Liquor Brewing

Duan Zhaofa was born in 1967, a native of Jieshou city, Anhui province. He is the founder of Jinyu Wan Liquor, senior liquor brewer, standing director of Anhui Liquor Association, and 9th national "star of entrepreneurship". Now, he is the chairman of Anhui Jinyu Wan Liquor Industry Co., Ltd.

Duan Zhaofa innovated the raw material, formula and techniques through the introduction of the "five-cereal brewing technology". Then he redetermined the brewing into 69 processes, making the "five-cereal brewing technology" become the first product in the Central Plains. The liquor produced by this technology can be divided into three types, namely, 42-degree liquor, 52-degree liquor, and 60-degree liquor. The brewed wine is clear and transparent with a long-standing aroma. You can feel sweet and smooth when you taste it, feel clean when it slips into your throat. With harmonious and perfect flavors, the brewed wine has been the very top of Luzhou-flavor Daqu liquor. In 2010, Jinyu Wan Liquor was recognized as "green food" by the Ministry of Agriculture. In 2012, it also won the title of "provincial new product". In 2014, Jinyu Wan trademark was recognized as "Anhui Time-honored Brand".

In May 2019, Duan Zhaofa entered the sixth list of province-level intangible cultural heritage representative heritors of Jinyu Wan Liquor Brewing.

Yingzhou Pillow Steamed Bun (province-level)

Hong Liangjun (province-level) | related item: Yingzhou Pillow Steamed Bun

Hong Liangjun was born in 1965. He is a Hui nationality and native of Fuyang city. He is a representative figure of famous food "Pillow Steamed Bun" of Fuyang city.

Since 1978, Hong Liangjun has studied to make pillow steamed bun from his father. He not only mastered the traditional techniques of pillow steamed bun making, but also kept innovating in practice. From 1990, he did this business independently with his own brand called "Honghuzi Pillow Steamed Bun".

After 30 years of exploration, Hong Liangjun has formed unique skills in the production of pillow steamed bun. For example, he kneads the dough without adding alkali and baking powder, which can help buns avoid being moldy or hard after several days of storage with the same fresh taste like before. The shape of the steamed bun is beautiful. The bottom of steamed bun is golden yellow, which looks like fried with about half an inch thick. Cutting a slice of it, you can see the bun is white and packed layer by layer. The bun is not dry and easy to chew because of its softness and good texture.

In 1996, the program "around the country" of CCTV reported "Honghuzi Pillow Steamed Bun", and the program "Zhengda variety show" also made a special report about him. In 2008, *"Reader Digest of Country' s Edition"* illustrated the production techniques of "Honghuzi Pillow Steamed Bun". In 2009, Hong Liangjun won the special contribution award in "China's First Buns Art Festival". In 2008, "Honghuzi Pillow Steamed Bun" was awarded the title of "Anhui time-honored brand" by the Department of Commerce of Anhui province. At the same year, his company was awarded the title of "top ten landmark food representative brand enterprises of Fuyang city, Anhui province" at the 8th China Anhui Cuisine Expo. Under the influence and drive of Hong Liangjun, "Fuyang Steamed Bun" went to the whole country, which not only satisfied people's daily consumption, but also became a good gift.

In May 2019, Hong Liangjun entered the sixth list of province-level intangible cultural heritage representative heritors of Yingzhou Pillow Steamed Bun.

Seven Quyi

Taihe Qinyin (province-level)

Zhang Hongkui (province-level) | related item: Taihe Qinyin

Zhang Hongkui was born in 1943, a native of Taihe county, Anhui province. He is the member of Anhui Theatre Association, director of Anhui Intangible Cultural Heritage Research Association and honorary chairman of Taihe Qingyin Association.

Zhang Hongkui studied with veteran Qingyin artists, such as Zhang Tianqing, Zhang Yalin and Zhang Junming. After joining the Qingyin Opera Troupe of Taihe county, he studied hard and gradually refined his acting skills. He once played as leading role in more than 20 large- and medium-sized Qingyin operas. His singing features are clear pronunciation, euphemistic style and proper cadence with good controlling on voice. His main plays include many modern plays, such as *Qingyin Praising the Flourishing Age, Gao Sijie, the Representative of the 19th National Congress of the Communist Party of China, Great and beautiful Taihe People, Celebrating the Birthday of New China*.

In his middle-aged and old life, Zhang Hongkui devoted himself to the spread work of "Qingyin". Since 2013, he has been teaching "Qingyin class" in Northern Anhui Electronic Information Engineering School. He has made a positive contribution to the inheritance and development of Taihe Qingyin.

In November 2008, Zhang Hongku entered the second list of province-level intangible cultural heritage representative heritors of Taihe Qinyin.

Xie Shuying (province-level) | related item: Taihe Qinyin

Xie Shuying was born in 1945, a native of Taihe county, Fuyang city. She has been engaged in the performance of Taihe Qingyin since 1958 and retired in 2000. She is a performing artist of Taihe Qingyin.

Xie Shuying studied from two famous Qingyin artists, Li Zicun and Zhang Junming, focusing on Hua Dan (a kind of female role in Chinese opera) and Guimen Dan (young and unmarried lady role in Chinese opera). In the treatment of singing melody, she has unique techniques with distinctive characteristics. Her singing is full of flexibility with a variety of different singing methods. Her performance is serious and delicate. The characters she performed are smart and close to life; Her tune is clear, with smooth switch between euphemistic high and low voices. She can control the speed of her singing and combine with her emotion and situation, which is widely welcomed by the audience.

In 1958, Xie Shuying took part in the provincial art performance and won the first prize for her role as matchmaker in the traditional play *Torturing the Matchmaker*. Her performance photos were included in the *Chinese Theater Dictionary*. In 1959, she won the first prize in the art performance in military district through playing the character Xiaoli (a female role) in the modern play *Mother-in-law and Daughter-in-law Sending Letters*. Then she was selected to take part in art performance of military district in Hefei city in the same year and won the first prize of individual performance. She once gave a special Qingyin performance for Dong Biwu, the former vice-president, and was cordially received by the state leaders at that time.

In May 2019, Xie Shuying entered the sixth list of province-level intangible cultural heritage representative heritors of Taihe Qinyin.

Jieshou Yugu (province-level)

Miao Qingchen (province–level) | related item: Jieshou Yugu

Miao Qingchen was born in 1943, a native of Renzhai village of Jieshou city, Anhui province. He is the member of Anhui Ballad Singers Association and famous performer of Yugu.

Miao Qingchen studied with Xu Zhibang, a Yugu artist. His singing features are distinctive, mainly with a slightly hoarse voice. His performance is magnificent with clear pronunciation and powerful voice. Sometimes he uses some singing techniques such as shanban (singing from unaccented beat) and duozi (singing lyrics before strong beat coming) to attract audience. In 2005, his Yugu work *Rural Credit Cooperatives Are Our Strong Backer* won the third prize in the Third Anhui Culture and Art Festival. In 2016, he participated in the premiere of Anhui station in the fifth and sixth programs of the second season of "Ding Luo Long Dong Qiang", a show produced by CCTV-3. In the programs, he performed the songs *The Last Blossom* and *La Muse de la nuit* with pop singer Shang Wenjie, which were highly praised by the audience.

In November 2008, Miao Qingchen entered the second list of province-level intangible cultural heritage representative heritors of Jieshou Yugu.

Shoulder Pole Show (province-level)

Zhu Yunde (province-level) | related item: Shoulder Pole Show

Zhu Yunde was born in 1952, a native of Lucun town of Jieshou city, Anhui province. He is the representative heritor of Jieshou Shoulder Pole Show.

Zhu Yunde studied from Zhu Huixian. He can use both hands and feet to complete a show by himself. His artistic features are clear pronunciation and beautiful singing. During the performance, he can whistle with copper in his mouth. His timbre is rich and delicate. He is good at simulating human voice, various animal calls, and various people's tones.

His representative plays include *Wang Xiaoer Selling Tofu*, *Wang Xiaoer Beating Tiger*, *Xianglian Suing*, *Ma Hulun Exchanging Marriage*, *Journey to the West*, *Piggie Carrying His Wife*, etc. In 2010, his repertoire, *Wang Xiaoer Beating Tiger* won award in the Fourth Anhui Quyi Festival.

In January 2011, Zhu Yunde entered the third list of province-level intangible cultural heritage representative heritors of Shoulder Pole Show.

Huai River Qinshu (province-level)

Cao Honghai (province–level) | related item: Huai River Qinshu

Cao Honghai was born in 1945, a native of Funan county, Anhui province. He is the former president of Quyi Association of Funan county, and representative heritor of Huai River Qinshu.

Since childhood, Cao Honghai learned to sing bass drum storytelling from Zhu Xiuchuan, a veteran artist. In 1964, he learned to sing Huai River Qinshu from Chen Zhimin. Later, he was personally instructed by the master Li Jiasheng. His artistic level is comprehensive. His singing is loud and deep, with old tunes and strong charm. His main representative works include *The Story of Wang Baotong*, *Generals of the Xue Family*, *Generals of the Yang Family*, *Records of Sui and Tang Dynasties*, *Ten Gold Fans* and so on. The traditional short play *Twelve Monks' Performance* won the second prize in the Second Northern Anhui Folk Art Competition.

In March 2015, Cao Honghai entered the fifth list of province-level intangible cultural heritage representative heritors of Huai River Qinshu.

Meng Ying (province-level) | related item: Huai River Qinshu

Meng Ying was born in 1973, a native of Funan county, Anhui province. She is the member of Chinese Ballad Singers Association and chairman of Anhui Ballad Singers Association. She is a national first-grade actor who enjoys special allowance from the State Council.

At the age of 7, Meng Ying learned to sing Qinshu with her father. At the age of 8, she began to perform with adults nationwide. In her nearly 40 years of artistic career, she has won many national and provincial awards. In 2004, she won the 3th "peony award", the highest award of Chinese Quyi; In 2013, she went to France for cultural exchange performance on behalf of China; In 2015, she won the top talent award in the field of propaganda and culture (literature and art) of Anhui province; In 2015, she won the first prize in the Quyi competition held by six central provinces; In 2016, she won the 17th "stars award", the highest award of The Ministry of Culture. In addition, she was also named as "the most beautiful grassroots cultural person" and one of the ten "representative figures" commended by the Publicity Department of Anhui province in 2018.

Over the years, Meng Ying has been sticking to the rural stage in order to display the new era and promote positive energy. She has created and sung many works that reflect the thoughts and feelings of grassroots people, such as *Buying a Slap*, *Happy Events*, *Neighborhoods*, *Nightmare*, *The Story of Rolling a Dog* and *Talking about New Changes in Rural Areas*. They are widely influential and popular among the masses.

In March 2015, Meng Ying entered the fifth list of province-level intangible cultural heritage representative heritors of Huai River Qinshu.

Yingshang Bass Drum Storytelling (province-level)

Zhang Jinpeng (province-level) | related item: Yingshang Bass Drum Storytelling

Zhang Jinpeng, stage name: "Zhang Minggui", was born in 1946 and died in 2018. He is the representative heritor of "Chaimen Bass Drum" of Yingshang Bass Drum Storytelling.

Zhang Jinpeng's words is humorous and pungent, with rich expressions and good use of dialects and idioms. His singing style absorbs the characteristics of "four-sentence tui opera" in Yingshang local operas as well as the singing characteristics of Qinshu, Shandong Kuaishu (narrative-singing), Henan Opera and other performing arts. His singing is in rhyme with high-pitched voice, meeting both refined and popular tastes, which is beautiful and full of charm. In terms of singing method, he mainly uses "hoarse voice" with strong timbre. His voice is rough and bold with hard, real and accurate pronunciation. He is likely to stop singing with a falling tone. The songs he sings are in dense words and fast speed. He is also good at using pause sound. All of these forms his unique singing style of winding flow tune, proper cadence, deep sound and strong emotion. In the performance, he is good at using hand method, eye method, body method and gait. In such performances as *Dragonfly Skimming the Water Surface, Hold the Moon in Arms, Wind Filling the Ears, Overlord lifting the Vessel, Su Qin Carrying Sword on His Back*, Zhang Jinpeng can not only gather the good sides of many schools, but also continuously develop and innovate the words, drums and tunes, which is deeply loved by the audience.

In March 2015, Zhang Jinpeng entered the fifth list of province-level intangible cultural heritage representative heritors of Yingshang Bass Drum Storytelling.

Yao Xinwen (province–level) | related item: Yingshang Bass Drum Storytelling

Yao Xinwen, stage name: "zuodipao", was born in 1944, a native of Runhe town of Yingshang county. He is the representative heritor of Yingshang Bass Drum Storytelling.

In 1961, Yao Xinwen studied from Lv Chuanbin, a famous artist of Yingshang Bass Drum Storytelling. In1963, he began to perform Yingshang Bass Drum Storytelling independently. His "unique skill" is to beat the drum with one hand and hit the board with the other. He tells stories in his loud voice, supplemented with wonderful narration, mellow singing, vivid imitation, and witty talking, which makes the performance lifelike. Although bass drum storytelling is an oral literature, he can change a wonderful story into an unforgettable performance through his mouth, which makes the audience feel like they are in the story. The performance is also very popular.

In March 2015, Yao Xinwen entered the fifth list of province-level intangible cultural heritage representative heritors of Yingshang Bass Drum Storytelling.

Lu Zhanjun (province-level) | related item: Yingshang Bass Drum Storytelling

Lu Zhanjun, stage name: "dagujiang", was born in 1947, a native of Yingshang county. He is the fourth-generation heritor of Yingshang Bass Drum Storytelling.

Lu Zhanjun started to learn this art in 1964. Under the guidance of his teacher, his narrative-singing became more and more proficient. His voice is loud with clear pronunciation. His tune is full of charm. His performance is vivid and natural. He could also perform different roles according to the actual scene and his own actions. In terms of singing method, he mainly uses "hoarse voice" with strong timbre. His voice is rough and bold with hard, real and accurate pronunciation. He is likely to stop singing with a falling tone. The songs he sings are in dense words and fast speed. He is also good at using pause sound. All of these forms his unique singing style of winding flow tune, proper cadence, deep sound and strong emotion. In the performance, he is good at using hand method, eye method, body method and gait. In such performances as *Dragonfly Skimming the Water Surface*, *Hold the Moon in Arms*, *Wind Filling the Ears*, *Overlord lifting the Vessel*, *Su Qin Carrying Sword on His Back*, he can not only gather the good sides of many schools, but also continuously develop and innovate the words, drums and tunes.

In May 2019, Lu Zhanjun entered the sixth list of province-level intangible cultural heritage representative heritors of Yingshang Bass Drum Storytelling.

Eight Folklore

Linquan Taige and Zhouge (province-level)

Liu Wenchang (state-level) I related item: Linquan Taige and Zhouge

Liu Wenchang was born in 1951, a native of Yangqiao town of Linquan county, Anhui province. He is a performing artist of Taige and Zhouge.

Liu Wenchang loved folk culture when he was young, with special preference for Taige and Zhouge in his hometown. When he was 4 years old, he took part in the performance with his uncle held by local Taige and Zhouge class. In his childhood, he performed some characters in such plays as *Journey to the West*, *Water Margin* and *Romance of the Three Kingdoms*. His performances were well-received.

Later, Liu Wenchang concentrated on the study of art creation and handcraft, which laid a good foundation for his further performance in Taige and Zhouge. Through active research and practice, his performance level has been greatly improved. The representative plays include *Liu Hai Playing with Golden Toads*, *Liu Quan Buying Watermelon*, *Three Kingdoms*, *Playing Peony* and *Traveling around the West Lake*, which have a great influence in the local area. He also got inspiration from modern and contemporary literary works and created a number of modern programs, such as *The Wreath Under the Mountain*, *The Bay of Liu River*, *Family Planning*, which also bring new vitality to this ancient art.

Liu Wenchang attaches great importance to the cultivation of folk art talents, and actively promotes the inheritance of Taige and Zhouge. Over the past few decades, he has cultivated a large number of new talents, making this old dance art with folk characteristics spread in Linquan county for a long time.

In May 2009, Liu Wenchang entered the third list of province-level intangible cultural heritage representative heritors of Linquan Taige and Zhouge.

Ding Yuxiang (province-level) | related item: Linquan Taige and Zhouge

Ding Yuxiang was born in 1945, a native of Zhangguan town of Linquan county, Anhui province. He is the second-generation heritor of Linquan Taige and Zhouge.

Since childhood, Ding Yuxiang has loved folk art very much. He is good at binding shelf of the Zhouge and proficient in various skills on the decoration of the shelf. The "shelf" created from his hands is firm, beautiful, practical, which provides a safe and pleasant environment for the young actor to perform. Ding Yuxiang is very fond of innovating Taige and Zhouge. He has created many new plays such as *Family Planning* and *Migrant Workers* based on the traditional plays which include *Liu Hai Playing with Golden Toads*, *Liu Quan Buying Watermelon*, *Monkey King Stealing Peach*, *Celestial Beauty Scattering Flowers*, *Three Kingdoms* and *Water Margin*. These plays are well-received.

Under his leadership for many years, the number of performance teams of Linquan Taige and Zhouge has grown from one to three, and the staff has increased from 60 to more than 200. From 2009 to 2017, he participated in the opening ceremony performance of the Anhui Folk Acrobatics Festival for four times. He also participated in more than 100 provincial and municipal large-scale performances and more than 300 commercial performances, which enriched the spiritual and cultural life of farmers.

In June 2011, Ding Yuxiang entered the fourth list of province-level intangible cultural heritage representative heritors of Linquan Taige and Zhouge.

Zhang Haimin (province-level) | related item: Linquan Taige and Zhouge

Zhang Haimin was born in 1953, a native of Linquan county, Anhui province. He is the representative heritor of Linquan Taige and Zhouge.

In 1982, Zhang Haimin studied from Zhang Xuezhong in the Taige and Zhouge team of Yangqiao town to learn the techniques of binding the costume, tiling the shelf and pile jacking. Later, he joined the performance team of Linquan Taige and Zhouge. Through hard study and practice, he mastered great skills and become the backbone of the local performance team.

His representative plays include *Liu Hai Playing with Golden Toads*, *Playing Peony* and *Traveling around the West Lake*. He participated in the opening ceremony of the National Farmers' Sports Meeting, the opening ceremony of the Second National Farmers' Song Festival (held in Chuzhou city) and the Spring Festival Gala of Anhui province. He has performed more than 300 times in various cities and counties, which is deeply loved by the audience. His wonderful performance has also been reported by CCTV and Anhui TV Station.

In March 2015, Zhang Haimin entered the fifth list of province-level intangible cultural heritage representative heritors of Linquan Taige and Zhouge.

Yingzhou Zhouge (province-level)

Li Deming (province-level) | related item: Yingzhou Zhouge

Li Deming was born in 1957. He is the province-level intangible cultural heritage representative heritor of Yingzhou Zhouge.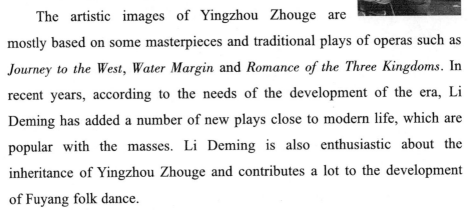

Since 1982, Li Deming has been engaged in the creation and performance of traditional folk dance. Through painstaking exploration and protection, he has organized and created a number of folk traditional plays of Zhouge with local traditional characteristics, which are deep loved by the masses.

The artistic images of Yingzhou Zhouge are mostly based on some masterpieces and traditional plays of operas such as *Journey to the West, Water Margin* and *Romance of the Three Kingdoms*. In recent years, according to the needs of the development of the era, Li Deming has added a number of new plays close to modern life, which are popular with the masses. Li Deming is also enthusiastic about the inheritance of Yingzhou Zhouge and contributes a lot to the development of Fuyang folk dance.

In January 2011, Li Deming entered the third list of province-level intangible cultural heritage representative heritors of Yingzhou Zhouge.

Zhang Clan Ancestral Hall Worship (province-level)

Zhang Shilin (province-level) | related item: Zhang Clan Ancestral Hall Worship

Zhang Shilin was born in 1950, a native of the Xingzheng village of Tanpeng town, Linquan county. He is the representative heritor of Zhang Clan Ancestral Hall Worship Activities.

Since 2006, Zhang Shilin organized and participated in the activities of cultural relics protection and worship ceremony in Zhang Clan Ancestral Hall. After years of efforts, Zhang Clan Ancestral Hall was listed as a key cultural relic protection unit at the county level by the county government in 2010. And in 2012, it was listed as a key cultural relic protection unit at the province level by Anhui Province People's Government. The ancestral hall was also renovated.

At the same time, Zhang Shilin conducted further research on the ancestral hall culture, the development history of the Zhang clan and the family cultural history. He organized several seminars attended by nearly 100 people, and went to many places to investigate and explore the development of the Zhang clan so as to sort out the follow-up work of family precepts, genealogy and worship activities.

In May 2019, Zhang Shilin entered the third list of province-level intangible cultural heritage representative heritors of Zhang Clan Ancestral Hall Worship Activities

Nine Folk Literature

Legend of Guan Zhong (province-level)

Feng Chuanli (province-level) | related item: Legend of Guan Zhong

Feng Chuanli was born in 1941, a native of Gungu village of Jianying town, Yingshang county, Anhui province. He is the representative heritor of Legend of Guan Zhong.

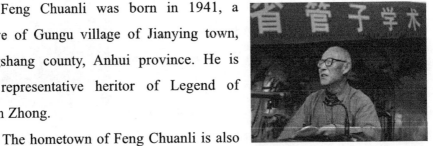

The hometown of Feng Chuanli is also the hometown of Guanzi. There are many historical legends about Guanzhong and Bao Shuya in Gungu village of Yingshang county. For the admiration for the sages of his hometown, Feng Chuanli often regretted the lack of records of Guanzhong and Bao Shuya's deeds in historical books. Therefore, he sprouted his ambition to collect, excavate and sort out their anecdotes, and firmly chose the hard road of studying Guanzi.

From the age of 40, Feng Chuanli went to the countrysides to collect the stories and legends handed down from mouth to mouth among the local people. He has persisted in this road for more than 30 years, accumulating day by day and writing incessantly. In the end, fruitful results have been achieved in the collation and promotion of the Legend of Guan Zhong.

In January 2011, Feng Chuanli entered the third list of province-level intangible cultural heritage representative heritors of Legend of Guan Zhong.

Gong Wu (province-level) | related item: Legend of Guan Zhong

Gong Wu was born in 1955, a native of Yingshang county, Anhui province. Now, he is the executive vice president and secretary general of Anhui Guanzi Research Association and chief editor of *Guanzi Research*.

Since 2000, Gong Wu has devoted himself to telling and popularizing the story of "Legend of Guan Zhong" in various ways, and has published nearly 8 million words of relevant articles. Among them, there are about 100 articles about Legend of Guan Zhong, studies of Guan Zhong and Guan Zhong culture. His monographs include *Meditation on Beauty*, *The Way of Guanzi's Governance*, *The Biography of Guanzi* (the cultural project of Anhui province), etc.; His anthologies include *Yingshang Historical and Cultural Collection*, *Analects on Studies of Guan Zhong*, *Treatise on Studies of Guan Zhong (volume 1-5)*, *New Treatise on Studies of Guan Zhong (volume 1-3)*, *The Contemporary Significance of Famous Chancellor Guanzi and His Thoughts*, etc.

Gong Wu's earliest work *On Guan Zhong's Birth in 723 BC* which tells stories of Guan Zhong and propagates Guan Zhong culture won the excellent achievement award of Anhui Federation of Social Sciences; *The Contemporary Significance of Famous Chancellor Guanzi and His Thoughts* won the first prize of excellent achievement award of studies of Guan Zhong in 2012; *The Philosophy of Guanzi's "Form, Situation and Doctrine" and Political Economy of "Light and Heavy Theory"* won the first prize of excellent achievement award of studies on Guan Zhong in 2019. He has been interviewed by CCTV for two consecutive years from 2018 to 2019 as the "spokesperson of Guan Zhong Culture", and has made positive contributions to the spread of Guan Zhong's stories and the promotion of Guan Zhong's moral thought and governance strategy in the contemporary era.

In May 2019, Gong Wu entered the sixth list of province-level intangible cultural heritage representative heritors of Legend of Guan Zhong.

List of Intangible Cultural Heritage Items in city-level and county-level

Number	Item name	Category	Place	Approval time
1	Liu Ling——Legend of Zuisan Qiu Liquor	Folk Literature	Fuyang city	2013
2	Legend of Wenwang Gong Liquor	Folk Literature	Linquan county	2013
3	Legend of Jiang Ziya	Folk Literature	Linquan county	2013
4	Legend of Gan Luo	Folk Literature	Yingshang county	2013
5	Xiyang Gong–drum	Traditional Music	Taihe county	2013
6	Lion Lantern Dance	Traditional Dance	Yingdong district	2007
7	Driving Stubborn Donkey Dance	Traditional Dance	Yingdong district	2007
8	Dragon Dance	Traditional Dance	Yingdong district	2013
9	Sanxianhui Dance	Traditional Dance	Yingzhou district	2020
10	Sanxianhui Dance	Traditional Dance	Funan county	2020
11	Huatiao Dance	Traditional Dance	Funan county	2010
12	Linquan Bang Opera	Traditional Opera	Linquan county	2016

Continued

Number	Item name	Category	Place	Approval time
13	Yingzhou Huai Tune	Quyi	Yingzhou district	2020
14	Funan Huai Tune	Quyi	Funan county	2020
15	Linquan Bass Drum Storytelling	Quyi	Linquan county	2020
16	Bass Drum Storytelling	Quyi	Funan county	2020
17	Huai Tune	Quyi	Fuyang city	2020
18	Yingzhou Bass Drum Storytelling	Quyi	Yingzhou district	2020 ·
19	Jieshou Square Chess	Traditional Sports, Entertainment and Aerobatics	Jieshou city	2013
20	Ying–Yang Eight–strength Hammer	Traditional Sports, Entertainment and Aerobatics	Yingzhou district	2020
21	Zhang Style Boxing	Traditional Sports, Entertainment and Aerobatics	Yingzhou district	2020
22	Wang Style Qigong	Traditional Sports, Entertainment and Aerobatics	Yingzhou district	2020
23	Liangyi Boxing	Traditional Sports, Entertainment and Aerobatics	Jieshou city	2020

Continued

Number	Item name	Category	Place	Approval time
24	Liangyi Boxing	Traditional Sports, Entertainment and Aerobatics	Linquan county	2020
25	Folk Paper-cut	Traditional Art	Yingdong district	2007
26	Funan Daodao Black Pottery	Traditional Art	Funan county	2007
27	Taihe Paper-cut	Traditional Art	Taihe county	2007
28	Linquan Dough Model-ling	Traditional Art	Linquan county	2010
29	Jieshou Paper-cut	Traditional Art	Jieshou city	2010
30	Fuyang Colour Model-ling	Traditional Art	Fuyang city	2013
31	Yingshang Paper-cut	Traditional Art	Yingshang county	2013
32	Jieshou Bamboo Weav-ing	Traditional Art	Jieshou city	2013
33	Beizhao Ancient Pottery	Traditional Art	Yingdong district	2016
34	Fuyang Pyrography	Traditional Art	Yingdong district	2016
35	Jieshou Wood Engraving	Traditional Art	Jieshou city	2016

Continued

Number	Item name	Category	Place	Approval time
36	Sand Calligraphy	Traditional Art	Linquan county	2020
37	Egg Engraving	Traditional Art	Linquan county	2020
38	Woodblock Lunar New Year Picture	Traditional Art	Jieshou city	2020
39	Jieshou Fish Print	Traditional Art	Jieshou city	2020
40	Jade Seal Engraving	Traditional Art	Yingzhou district	2020
41	Wang Guoqing Miniature Engraving	Traditional Art	Yingzhou district	2020
42	Miniature Engraving	Traditional Art	Yingquan district	2020
43	Gourd Pyrography	Traditional Art	Yingquan district	2020
44	Gaomiao Shajiang	Traditional Art	Taihe county	2020
45	Damiao Gourd Pyrography	Traditional Art	Taihe county	2020
46	Tiger–like Shoe	Traditional Craftsmanship	Yingquan district	2007
47	Wood Engraving	Traditional Craftsmanship	Linquan county	2007
48	Gaotang Baimeidou	Traditional Craftsmanship	Linquan county	2010

Continued

Number	Item name	Category	Place	Approval time
49	Taihe Gongchun	Traditional Craftsmanship	Taihe county	2010
50	Fangji Sanzi	Traditional Craftsmanship	Funan county	2016
51	Yingling Crisp Cake	Traditional Craftsmanship	Linquan county	2016
52	Lv Changming Braised Beef	Traditional Craftsmanship	Jieshou city	2016
53	Fuyang Crisp Burnt Bun	Traditional Craftsmanship	Yingzhou district	2020
54	Li Jinling Mounting of Calligraphy and Painting	Traditional Craftsmanship	Yingzhou district	2020
55	Wang Hai Restoration of Ancient Calligraphy and Painting	Traditional Craftsmanship	Yingzhou district	2020
56	Yanlong Tribute Oil	Traditional Craftsmanship	Yingzhou district	2020
57	Steelyard	Traditional Craftsmanship	Funan county	2020
58	Pork Knuckle and Meat	Traditional Craftsmanship	Yingdong district	2020
59	Fentai Mung Bean Balls	Traditional Craftsmanship	Taihe county	2020
60	Chuantuo	Traditional Craftsmanship	Linquan county	2020

Continued

Number	Item name	Category	Place	Approval time
61	Lilao village Pot-stewed Pig Feet	Traditional Craftsmanship	Linquan county	2020
62	Northern Anhui Shepherd's Purse	Traditional Craftsmanship	Linquan county	2020
63	Translucent Sheep's Hooves	Traditional Craftsmanship	Linquan county	2020
64	Chunfeng Donkey Meat	Traditional Craftsmanship	Jieshou city	2020
65	Jieshou Crusty Pancake	Traditional Craftsmanship	Jieshou city	2020
66	Sanhuaitang Bean Vermicelli	Traditional Craftsmanship	Jieshou city	2020
67	Heiao Zi Liquor	Traditional Craftsmanship	Jieshou city	2020
68	Qianyuan Studio Brush	Traditional Craftsmanship	Jieshou city	2020
69	Li Liangcheng Smoked Chicken	Traditional Craftsmanship	Jieshou city	2020
70	Jieshou Clothes Weaving	Traditional Craftsmanship	Jieshou city	2020
71	Chen Style Sheet Jelly	Traditional Craftsmanship	Jieshou city	2020
72	Wu Style Hands Diagnosis and Therapy	Traditional Medicine	Yingdong district	2010
73	Qin Style Burn Prescription	Traditional Medicine	Linquan county	2010

Continued

Number	Item name	Category	Place	Approval time
74	Pearl and Cow Bezoar Powder Prescription	Traditional Medicine	Linquan county	2020
75	Wangshoutang Traditional Chinese Medicine Processing	Traditional Medicine	Funan county	2020
76	Wadian Town Sheepfight	Folklore	Linquan county	2013
77	Yingnan Folk Art Fair	Folklore	Jieshou city	2016

Postscript

Through relentless efforts of extensively collecting materials and editing for several times, Bureau of Culture, Tourism and Sports of Fuyang and Fuyang Intangible Cultural Heritage Protection Center finally finished this book, *Illustrated Collection of Fuyang Intangible Cultural Heritage*. This book aims at the publicity, promotion and display of intangible cultural heritage items and representative heritors in Fuyang city comprehensively. The compilation and publication of this book also has several reasons. The first is to thoroughly implement the spirit of a series of important speeches delivered by general secretary Xi Jinping on inheriting and developing the fine traditional Chinese culture. The second is to implement the relevant requirements of *Opinions on Implementing the Inheritance and Development of Chinese Traditional Culture* issued by the General Office of the CPC Central Committee and the General Office of the State Council and further propagandize and implement *Intangible Cultural Heritage Law of the People's Republic of China*. The third is to promote the protection and inheritance of intangible cultural heritage in Fuyang and its creative transformation and innovative development on intangible cultural heritage to realize sustainable protection. The fourth is to further display the rich resources of intangible cultural heritage in Fuyang. The fifth is to carry out the rescue recording work of representative heritors and guide them to actively implement inheritance activities. By doing so, the public opinions and good ethos on attaching importance to the protection and inheritance of intangible cultural heritage can be formed.

We would like to express our heartfelt thanks to the leaders at all levels who have attached great importance to and wholeheartedly supported to the protection and inheritance of intangible cultural heritage in Fuyang for many years, to the people from all walks of life who have done a lot of work for the protection and inheritance of intangible cultural heritage in all cities, districts and counties, to Anhui Xinhua Electronic Audiovisual Press, to Mr. Xing Sijie and student Beichen for coordinating, revising and proofreading the manuscript, and to all those who have worked hard for this book.

General secretary Xi Jinping pointed out that the prosperity of a state and a nation is always supported by its cultural prosperity. The great rejuvenation of the Chinese nation requires the development and prosperity of Chinese culture. Intangible cultural heritage is the cultural mark of a nation and the way of life of a nation and a region. The protection and inheritance of intangible cultural heritage has a long way to go with a glorious mission. The bright light of civilization illuminates the road of national rejuvenation. We will strive to build a great and beautiful city in terms of protection and inheritance of intangible cultural heritage in line with the direction pointed out by general secretary Xi Jinping for the protection of cultural and natural heritage, strive to promote the deep integration of intangible cultural heritage and tourism, and constantly satisfy people's yearning for a beautiful and happy life.

Editor